# Ken Stabler's
# winning offensive football

**Introduction by Paul (Bear) Bryant**

**Ken Stabler** with Tom LaMarre

Henry Regnery Company • Chicago

**Library of Congress Cataloging in Publication Data**

Stabler, Ken.
    Winning offensive football.

    Includes index.
    1.   Football—Offense.    I.    LaMarre, Tom, joint
author.    II.   Title.
GV951.8.S7    1976      796.33′22      76-20694
ISBN 0-8092-7991-6
ISBN 0-8092-7990-8 pbk.

Cover photograph by Arthur Anderson
Photos by Russ Reed, Arthur Anderson, Mervyn Lew,
Vernon J. Biever, Dave Karp, Compix, Inc.

Published by Henry Regnery Company
180 North Michigan Avenue, Chicago, Illinois 60601
Manufactured in the United States of America
Library of Congress Catalog Card Number: 76-011227
International Standard Book Number: 0-8092-7991-6 (cloth)
                                   0-8092-7990-8 (paper)

Published simultaneously in Canada by
Beaverbooks
953 Dillingham Road
Pickering, Ontario L1W 1Z7
Canada

# contents

# introduction

*By Paul (Bear) Bryant*
*Head Football Coach, University of Alabama*

Looking back, I remember that the first time I really watched Kenny Stabler play a football game in person was in the Alabama high school all-star game in Tuscaloosa.

What I saw was a young man who was pencil-thin, who threw left-handed, and who did a great job in running the football and in directing his team to a victory.

When Kenny came to the University, he didn't weigh more than 165 pounds and, frankly, we were all a little concerned about whether he could stand the punishment of college football.

It was easy to see that he had talent. He had excellent timing, a football mind, the confidence of his teammates, and the ability to glide along with long strides that chewed up more yardage than you expected every time he ran the football.

I won't say we didn't have a few differences of opinion during the years he played at Alabama. We did. I had to discipline him once but I think it helped make him a better person. In any athletic program you have to have rules and regulations, and anyone who doesn't subscribe to those rules has to be disciplined. It doesn't matter if it is your star player, as it was in Kenny's case, or the last man on the roster. If you don't have discipline, you can't have a successful program.

I don't want to dwell on this, but I think it is important. Now I think Kenny will tell you he was wrong, and that youngsters reading his book should know that training rules are to be followed, even if you don't agree with them.

But enough about that. Kenny was and still is one of the finest quarterbacks I've ever seen play football. He had a grace and style all his own. He had that ability to turn a busted play into a big gainer, to make things happen.

I've been fortunate to have a lot of great quarterbacks in my coaching career. Kenny certainly ranks as one of the very best. No coach who has been in the business as long as I have would dare pick out any one individual as the "best" he has coached. It just wouldn't be fair to the others, and besides, it would make one guy happy and the rest mad at me.

But I'll have to say that for poise, guts, leadership, and the ability to run with the football and pass it with great accuracy under pressure, Kenny might just be the one quarterback I would pick if I had to name one at his peak to win a single game.

I remember a lot of great moments in his career with the Crimson Tide. His junior year, 1966, we had what I still consider the finest football team I've ever been associated with. We had won the national championship in 1964 and 1965, and in 1966 we stayed undefeated by wearing out a fine Nebraska team, 34-7, in the Sugar Bowl. Kenny had a lot of great games that year, but his play against Nebraska was really magnificent.

It would be impossible for any Alabama fan to forget Kenny's final regular-season game as a senior in 1967. We were playing arch rival Auburn in Birmingham back when they still had a grass field. It rained all night before the game and all during the game. The field was a complete sea of mud. It didn't look like either team would ever score.

We had the ball about midfield, when Kenny ran the option to the

right side (see photo). He got a block on the corner by Dennis Dixon, and when he turned downfield all I could think of was his being
wide open but slipping down in the mud. A couple of Auburn
players had a shot at making the tackle, but Kenny gave them his
famous hip fake and finally made it to the end zone, just stepping in
before a couple of Auburn players were all over him. I'm sure the
run didn't take more than six or seven seconds, but it seemed an
eternity.

We've all watched Kenny mature and develop into a great professional quarterback. He remains one of the most accurate passers
I've ever seen, with the ability to throw a "soft" pass that is easy to
catch.

Kenny also has done a fine job with his summer football camp for
youngsters, and has a charming, warm personality that makes it
possible for anyone to feel at ease around him. That, I think, is important in teaching youngsters the fundamentals of football.

I'm sure that if you will read and practice the various instruc-
tions in this book, you'll be a much sounder football player. Repetition is so important in football, so don't forget to keep working on
all phases of the game, even after you think you've mastered a particular one.

It may not make you a great player like Kenny Stabler, but it certainly will give you the opportunity to enjoy the game of football
and get some fun out of it.

# chapter one

# the evolution of offense

When you scan the annals of football history, one thing that becomes immediately evident is that the offense dominated the game from the beginning. For 50 or 60 years it was basically an offensive game, and offensive weapons were sometimes outlawed in order to keep somewhat of a balance between offense and defense. Today the game is specialized, with players learning one position and staying with it. In the old days, they put 11 guys on the field and you almost had to die to be replaced. A good player would stay on the field, no matter what, sometimes playing several positions in a game.

That meant that often players would loaf on defense and just wait to get back on offense again. If the other team scored, that was OK, because now we got the ball again and could get that score back.

1

Early football, as shown in this 1912 game between Harvard and Princeton, was much like hand-to-hand combat, until the pass was legalized in 1912. But notice the huge crowd, even in those days (UPI).

You just tried to score more points than the other team. It's amazing to me how some of those guys played so long. We have a lot of injuries sometimes with players going only one way. But 60 minutes of football without much equipment is something, and I'm sure the game was as rough then as it is now, even though the players weren't as big and maybe not as fast. It took a special breed of man, and there are some of those left today, but I don't see how you could do it today. Everyone plays half the time and is well rested. The last guy to go both ways was Philadelphia Eagles center-linebacker Chuck Bednarik in 1960, and they gave him breathers when they got ahead or in games against lesser opponents.

Since football evolved from rugby, the first formation or play of sorts was the scrum—just a mass of players fighting for the ball—but that was gone from the game by 1880. They used sort of a rough T, with line and backfield positions defined, but they didn't even get into stances. It was stand up and fight it out any way you could, sort of like hand-to-hand combat. Blocking rules weren't even defined yet, so you could hold and do almost anything else you wanted to an opponent. It wasn't until about the turn of the century that line play and blocking rules gained sophistication.

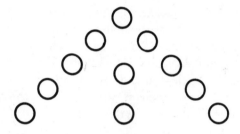

Diagram 1
Flying wedge

The first really big formation was the flying wedge (diagram 1), which was introduced about 1892, with both Harvard and Penn laying claim to that invention. Nine offensive players would form a V-formation by locking arms, with the ball carrier and another blocker inside, and take a 20-yard head start at the defense. Naturally, the effect of this play was devastating. We have a powerful offensive line with the Oakland Raiders, with guys like Art Shell and Gene Upshaw, and if we ran this play, even Mean Joe Greene and the Pittsburgh Steelers with the help of Minnesota's Purple Gang couldn't stop it. That play is a cinch to gain yards. But I know that you'd have a high injury factor involved. That's probably why the flying wedge and the v-trick, another formation in which blockers surrounded the ball carrier, were outlawed in 1894. That's the way they defensed things in those days.

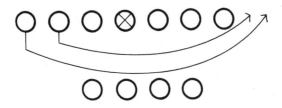

Diagram 2
Flying interference (rough T)

But you can see that coaches with football minds were constantly striving to find something to beat the defense, even in those days. Because the flying wedge was now illegal, Coach Woodruff at Penn invented what he called "flying interference" (diagram 2). On this play, the weak-side tackle and end would pull out of the line before the snap and run between the rest of the line and the backs. Just as the end and tackle reached the other side of the line, the ball was snapped and, with the other backs leading the way, the ball carrier had a wall of interference. It's incredible to me that a coach back then would think of this, because it's the same principle we use today when pulling linemen on sweeps and trap plays. That coach had no background to go with, it's just something that popped into his head. That was the first Green Bay Sweep or USC Student Body Right, some great modern-day football plays that we'll study later.

It was important to the development of football that there were inventive coaches like Woodruff, Amos Alonzo Stagg, and John Heisman in the early years. Stagg, who coached for 57 years until the mid-1950s, developed his "ends-back" formation to provide more blocking power, just as coaches will do today with two- and three-tight-end formations. He also began a wild-looking thing called the "turtleback," a revolving circle of blockers surrounding the ball carrier. You couldn't do some of these things now, because the linemen must be set in their stances and can't move until the ball is snapped, but these were ingenious designs for the times. Of course the back in the turtleback would be difficult to reach—plus you never knew when he was going to break out.

A lot of people these days don't know much about John Heisman, but when you check the football history books, it's easy to see why they named the trophy for the best college player in the country after him. He was a fine player at first, then one of football's early innovators. He invented the spinner, which is much like what the T-formation quarterback does on reverse pivot with faking and ball-handling. It was important to the single wing as well. Heisman was also the first to use laterals and the direct snap from center, both of which are integral parts of the game today. Because of brilliant men like this in the game's early stages, football is what it is nowadays.

The biggest thing, in my opinion, that happened to football—in the early years or in modern times—was the legalization of the forward pass in 1906. It's immeasurable what that's done for the game. At that time, what it did was open up football. It had been all running before that—a game only for the rugged, unless you had a breakaway runner. I can appreciate a tough, defensive game and a hard-hitting ground game, but as a steady diet this can be boring. I'm sure that without the passing game, football wouldn't have had the impact on the American public that it had and still has. I believe that football wouldn't have had such wide appeal if it was just a running game. If there were 60- or 70-yard runs all day long, the running game would be the same way. But there aren't. People can watch the passing game all day. Even an incomplete long passing play can be exciting. Or an interception.

There have been only a handful of guys in the history of football who drew people to see them run every time they played. There are many outstanding backs playing right now, but the only one, I think, who actually fits that description is O. J. Simpson. Among the others were Jim Thorpe (probably the first one), Red Grange, Jim Brown, Gale Sayers, and probably only a few others. When the Buffalo Bills play on television, I want to see O. J. run with the ball, but when Pittsburgh is on, I don't wait for them to give the ball to Franco Harris, although he is a fine back. I believe that most football observers feel the same way. There are many good backs, but only a few with that something special.

On the other hand, there have been hundreds of guys who were

Red Grange, the Galloping Ghost. He once ran for five touch-downs, four in the first 11 minutes of the game, and passed for another while accumulating 402 total yards (in the dedication game of Illinois' Memorial Stadium in 1924).

drawing cards because they threw the football. Probably the first one was Gus Dorais at Notre Dame in 1913, and perhaps only because his favorite receiver was a foresighted guy named Knute Rockne. Even though it had been legal for seven years, the pass was still used sparingly for the first several years. I can guess that the Carroll College team was pretty surprised when St. Louis passed for a touchdown in the first game in which the pass was legalized. But the major schools stuck with basically a running offense until that day when little Notre Dame met powerful unbeaten Army in New York. Rockne and Dorais had worked at a Lake Erie resort all summer, and had practiced the pass in their spare time. Army, which had an opening in its schedule and had invited the Fighting Irish east, was stunned 35-13 when Dorais completed 13 of 17 for 243 yards and a 25-yard touchdown to Rockne. Those statistics would make a present-day quarterback proud, but in those days

An early passing play, with Albie Booth of Yale throwing the ball in a 1931 game against Dartmouth.

they were unheard of. I wouldn't be at all surprised if it was Rockne who first saw the potential of the forward pass and said, "Hey, Gus, we've got to work on this," because Rockne later proved himself to be one of the great minds of football when he became coach at Notre Dame.

A year later came the "flea-flicker," a play that we still see today, but usually in a desperation situation. It's a surprise type of thing, with the quarterback handing off on what looks like a running play, taking a lateral from the back, and then throwing a pass. But the story in this era of football was the running of Jim Thorpe, the young Indian boy playing at the Carlisle Indian School. His team beat the national powerhouses, mainly on his long touchdown runs. He was football's first superstar.

Thorpe's coach at Carlisle was Pop Warner, who realized that with a great back like Thorpe, the thing to do was let him carry the ball as much as possible and give him every chance to break out into the open. Just a few years later, Warner would gain further fame,

7

Jim Thorpe of the Carlisle Indian School and later the Canton Bulldogs. He was probably the game's first real superstar.

now at Stanford on the West Coast, by designing the single wing (diagram 3). This would be the basic football formation for many years. But there were other vital occurrences during this period.

In 1915, Oklahoma was the new powerhouse from out West, going undefeated. That in itself wasn't so startling, but the way the Sooners did it was. They averaged 30 passes a game! Oklahoma has been a power for many years in modern football, but I don't think the modern Sooners ever threw that many passes in a game. Heck, most pro teams don't throw that much, but here was a team in 1915 doing it. Also around this time, Coach Bob Zuppke at Illinois devised the huddle and later the screen pass, both important parts of the game even today.

Though the college game was the heart of the game in those days, there had been professional games between town teams almost since

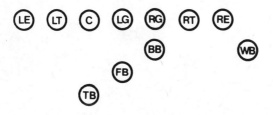

Diagram 3
Single wing

the beginning of the century. But in 1922, George Halas, still today the owner of the Chicago Bears and for a long time their coach after a fine playing career, got together with a group of other representatives from town teams and formed what would eventually be the National Football League. It took hold slowly, with much shuffling and struggling of franchises in the early years, as with many new leagues, but it survived to grow into the major sports empire that it is today.

As I pointed out, Pop Warner's single wing became the basic offense of the times. There are any number of combinations with the tailback and the fullback on spinners and fakes, plus the wingback coming back across on counters. The quarterback is strictly a blocking back, whereas today I rarely throw a block unless a situation arises in which I must, suddenly and surprisingly. I feel that I might have been the tailback, who was a runner and a passer, if I had played in this offense. But George Blanda was a blocking back in the single wing at Kentucky. With an unbalanced line, the single wing was a great running formation with seven blockers on the strong side of the formation. But I think when the defense stacked on the strong side, you could break long runs the other way with the wingback on counter plays. And since it was basically a running formation, I think that you could fake a run and get your pass receivers open for big plays. Somewhere along the line, they began to split one or both of the ends a bit in order to get them out on pass plays, and the wingback also was utilized as a receiver.

9

The workings of the single wing are shown by the 1944 University of Washington team. The single wing thrived for nearly 40 years (Acme Photo).

Knute Rockne, that first renowned pass receiver, developed one of the first extensions of the single wing when he introduced his Notre Dame box (diagram 4), which used shifting in the backfield for the first time. I don't know if it is true or not, but there is a romantic story about Rockne getting his inspiration for this when he watched a line of chorus girls dancing at a show he attended one night. In any case, the box shift moved the backs in the backfield at the last minute, leaving the defense very little time to adjust. With the line now balanced, you could switch the strong side of your formation right before the center snap, something that some modern teams do. Usually, the tailback was your best player, a runner and passer, but perhaps Rockne had another guy with many talents, because he used the wingback more than others had, moving him around and sending him out more on pass routes. The pros even picked up on this offense.

Many other formations came off the single wing, such as the Sutherland single wing and the New York Giants' A-formation. The Green Bay Packers used the single wing, but they had one of the great all-time receivers, Don Hutson, playing at end. That's

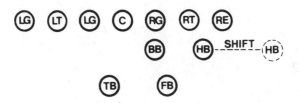

Diagram 4
Notre Dame box

when the single wing was more of a passing formation, because Hutson is still ranked right up there near the top 10 among the all-time receivers. But he still had to be a strong blocker because the single wing was a running offense. He probably would have been an even better receiver if he had been able to split out on every play and not have to worry about blocking at all. Mike Siani, one of our fine receivers with the Raiders, was an end in a single wing offense in high school. He's easily the best blocker among our receivers, and I'll bet it goes back to his days as a tight end in the single wing, though they split him out on passing plays. Don Hutson was probably the first great tight end, exceptional as a blocker and a receiver.

The single wing was used for 40 years at Tennessee, mostly under Colonel Bob Neyland, after whom Neyland Stadium in Knoxville was named. I remember seeing the Volunteers and Vanderbilt use it against Alabama when I was a kid. Johnny Majors, the coach at the University of Pittsburgh, was an All-American tailback at Tennessee, and I can recall seeing him play. It was played in major college football into the 1960s. Billy Kilmer, the quarterback of the Washington Redskins, was a single wing tailback at UCLA. And Oregon State, with Terry Baker at tailback the last three years, used it until 1962. I believe it's still used by some high schools today. It's an offense that endured over the years after Pop Warner

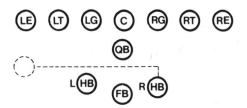

Diagram 5
T-formation

first used it. I can understand why they named a kids' football league after him.

But the offense that led to today's modern-day alignments is the T-formation (diagram 5). Coach Ralph Jones of the Chicago Bears introduced it to pro football in 1931 and while the college stayed with the single wing, the "T" revolutionized pro ball. This is when the rules of football were altered to take advantage of specialized talents. The biggest thing was that the quarterback could now throw from anywhere behind the line of scrimmage, instead of a designated spot five yards back. Roger Staubach, Fran Tarkenton, and today's other scramblers couldn't have done their thing in those days.

In addition to introducing the quarterback snap from center, the T-formation gave the offense more flexibility and the element of surprise. It allowed for more effective running fakes and gave the quarterback more time to pass. The running backs were now going nearly full speed when they hit the holes, whereas they were dead in their tracks when they got the ball in the single wing. Starting from deeper in the backfield, the backs could read the blocking combinations easier, and didn't need as good a block because they were running full speed when they passed a defender. It helped the passing game because it provided cup or pocket protection for the quarterback, in addition to the blockers in the backfield.

12

Clark Shaughnessy coaches his Stanford team of 1940 in the T-formation, the first college team to use it. That's Frankie Albert at left halfback; though he later was twice All-American quarterback.

Clark Shaughnessy introduced the T-formation to college ball at Stanford in the early 1940s, and he had a guy who had to be pretty good at it, Frankie Albert, since he was left-handed.

The Bears continued in the revolutionizing business in 1940 when they began sending a man in motion out of the backfield to get him into a pass route more quickly. They had a fine runner-receiver, George McAfee, at right halfback and they wanted to take advantage of both his talents. Also, the Bears had a great passer, Sid Luckman, and when they split out one end and sent McAfee in motion, it was the equivalent of today's pro set, which is our basic formation (diagram 6). Teams went along like this, sending backs in motion, for about 10 years until the Los Angeles Rams had a guy named Elroy (Crazylegs) Hirsch doing it, and finally the Rams just left him out there. That was the pro set to a T.

This was the era in which the passing game really began to flourish. There was one great quarterback after another. In addition to Luckman, there were Sammy Baugh, Bob Waterfield, Frankie

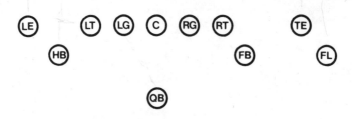

Diagram 6
Shotgun

Albert, Bobby Layne, Otto Graham, Eddie LeBaron, Norm Van Brocklin, Adrian Burk, Frank Tripuka, Babe Parilli, Tobin Rote, Chuck Connerly, and others. One of those others was Y. A. Tittle. In 1959, Coach Red Hickey introduced the shotgun (diagram 6) to pro football. This idea was probably taken from other formations, such as the single wing and the short punt. The San Francisco 49ers, in addition to having a fine passer in Tittle, had excellent receivers in the backfield with Hugh McElhenny and Joe Perry. McElhenny probably would have been one of the game's great receivers if he hadn't been such a great halfback. This formation put both McElhenny and Perry one step behind the tackles, in a slot inside both ends, with the flanker on one side or the other outside one of the ends.

The 49ers had two fine outside receivers, Billy Wilson and R. C. Owens, a former basketball player who made the "alley oop" pass famous, and tight end Clyde Conner. The 49ers used the shotgun as part of their offense for a few years, but in 1961, Hickey made it the basic San Francisco offense. The Niners rolled through the first five games with a 4-1 record, beating Washington 35-3, running over Detroit 49-0, tearing up Los Angeles 35-0, and pounding Minnesota 38-24. Tittle had been traded to the New York Giants, but Hickey shuttled three quarterbacks in the shotgun. He had John Brodie, a passer; Billy Kilmer, a runner; and Bobby Waters, a fine ball handler and adequate runner and passer. The 49ers went into Chicago to play the Bears, whose defensive coach was none other than Clark Shaughnessy, who devised a plan to stop the shotgun. He sent his linebacker on blitzes at the San Francisco quarterbacks, who were unprotected by running back blockers, and mixed up his defensive coverages to stymie the 49ers 31-0. Hickey junked the shotgun, even though it still appears as part of some teams' offense. But like anything else that features just the run or just the pass, it can be stopped.

At just about that same time, the Philadelphia Eagles had an awesome passing attack, which was beginning to see more and more zone pass coverage instead of just the man-to-man that teams had used for years. So, Coach Buck Shaw came up with the slot formation, which put both wide receivers on one side of the field. The Eagles put Tommy McDonald in the slot inside wide receiver Bobby Walston, with tight end Pete Retzlaff on the opposite side of the formation. This is what we do with Cliff Branch in the slot, Fred Biletnikoff outside, and our tight end on the other side in what we call our "east formation," which we'll go over in great detail later on. What it did for the Eagles was leave Retzlaff and Walston in one-on-one coverage, with Norm Van Brocklin throwing the ball. Van Brocklin still holds the record for most passing yards in one game, 540. This team could definitely move the ball, especially through the air. This was the only team to beat Vince Lombardi's Green Bay Packers in a Championship Game, and was the last really good Eagle team. There is opinion in some quarters that this is not a very good running formation, but the Eagles ran some out of it, and we've done an awful lot with it.

As you can see, this brings us into the era in which I began playing.

# chapter two

Right about the time I began playing high school football in Foley, Alabama, John McKay was taking flanker Willie Brown at the University of Southern California and putting him behind fullback Ben Wilson to form what resembled the letter "I," since both players were lined up behind the quarterback. That was the beginning of the I-formation, and USC has made a living from it since then. It was generally run out of the pro set (diagram 7) with the only adjustment made by the backs.

Brown, even though he was a coach for the Trojans for many years, has been all but forgotten because of the succession of famous tailbacks USC has lined up behind equally obscure fullbacks who blocked like nobody's business. Mike Garrett and O. J. Simpson won the Heisman Trophy from the USC tailback spot,

# offense since 1960

and Clarence Davis, Anthony Davis, and Ricky Bell piled up equally impressive totals running the ball.

The basic needs of the I-formation, which thrives on all levels of
football today, are an outstanding running back and a big, powerful
offensive line that specializes in man-to-man blocking. It opens up
both sides of the field to the tailback, who lines up seven full yards
behind the line of scrimmage, instead of the normal four. The back
just reads the holes developed by the line charge and picks the best
spot. You can run quick pitches and other plays to spring this back
into the open field quickly, but the play that USC specializes in is
called the blast (diagram 8).

The blast is basically an off-tackle, with the fullback leading
through the hole. And, as the name suggests, the offense team just

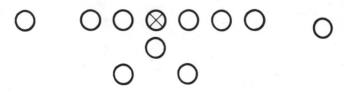

Diagram 7
Pro set

attempts to knock the defenders out of the way. That's a philosophy used by many teams, but it takes on another connotation when O.J. Simpson is carrying the ball. The Trojans also made famous their sweep, which used so many linemen pulling as blockers that it was dubbed "student body right or left."

The I-formation was the rage of the 1960s, especially in the college ranks. I ran it myself at Alabama, but we ran the option play off it most of the time. I'd fake into the line with the fullback and run down the line with the tailback trailing behind me. I'd either turn upfield myself or pitch out to the back at the last minute. Sometimes I'd fake to the fullback, pull up, and throw a quick pass to the tight end or something to one of my wide receivers, like a post pattern. It was a big part of our offense.

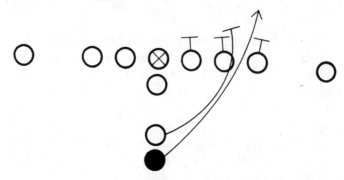

Diagram 8
I-formation (USC blast play)

● designates ball carrier

USC's I-formation, with O. J. Simpson lined up at tailback behind the quarterback and fullback (top). Coach John McKay used this as his bread-and-butter formation for 15 years, and made the Blast play (center) and the Student Body Sweep (bottom) famous with Simpson and an incredible string of other outstanding tailbacks.

19

This is the way we looked in the I-formation at Alabama in a 1967 game against Mississippi.

You still see the I-formation very much in football these days, but it's incorporated into an offense rather than being the main offensive formation. When Ohio State had Archie Griffin, they would put him in the I behind Pete Johnson or Champ Henson, two of those big fullbacks Woody Hayes always comes up with, and Archie ran to two Heismans that way. But the Buckeyes did some different things, too. Teams have to these days, to give defenses more to be concerned with. Defensive football has grown, so the offense has gone with it.

Pro teams run basically out of the pro set. They're going to come out with two wide receivers and split backs, because that's the ideal

We are about to line up in our double-tight-end formation. We are close to the goal and have come up to a short-yardage situation, needing only a couple of yards for a first down. We've inserted an extra tight end (No. 87, Dave Casper) in order for wide receiver Fred Biletnikoff to get more blocking power. We often go to three tight ends, taking out Cliff Branch (21), our other wide receiver.

formation for a passing team. But you'll see some I, a lot of shifts and men in motion, double wings, triple wings, three wide receivers, two tight ends, three tight ends, the slot formation, and even the old 49er shotgun occasionally.

In college football, where there is more running, the big thing these days is the triple-option. There are different varieties of this, such as the Texas wishbone and the veer-T. All three backs are in the backfield again. Heck, it wasn't that long ago that the old full-

21

Coach Hank Stram, regarded as one of football's great innovators, devised the moving pocket while at Kansas City. Quarterback Len Dawson takes a slight roll and stays in the pocket behind the tackle (in this case Dave Hill) instead of dropping straight back.

house backfield was used in pro football. Hank Stram, when he was at Kansas City, had his receivers all banged up one game, so he went back to the full-house and beat the Raiders 24-10 in 1968. Anything that can be done in football will be done.

Hank Stram is known as an innovator, and I believe that he relishes the title. Now the coach of the New Orleans Saints, he had great personnel with the Chiefs and always had them doing something different. In 1969, the year they went to the Super Bowl, Stram had what he called the "moving pocket." Instead of dropping straight back, quarterback Len Dawson would roll either right or left and the linemen would move with him. They knew he was going to be behind the tackle, so they blocked accordingly. It was good for Dawson, because it gave him extra time and he's adept at throwing on the move.

Stram always liked to move his offensive people around with shifts and motion before the play. He invented the tight-I (diagram 9), in which four men would be lined up behind the center. The tight end would be added to the conventional I right behind the quarterback. Most of the time, they'd shift out of this, with the tight end lining up in his normal position either left or right, but it gave the defense very little time to adjust. Sometimes, they'd run a play with him back there as an extra blocker. In the 1969 playoffs against the then-world champion New York Jets, Kansas City recovered the

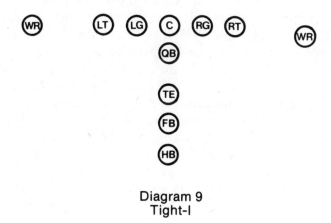

Diagram 9
Tight-I

opening kickoff and right away Stram went to his bag of tricks. He lined up wide receiver Otis Taylor in a gap between the guard and tackle on one side, and when the Jets couldn't find him, Taylor went downfield and caught a TD pass from Dawson on the first offensive play of the game. The Chiefs beat the Jets that day, the Raiders the next week, and went on to take the Vikings in the Super Bowl.

Hank Stram was acclaimed an offensive genius. *Sports Illustrated* ran a big article on his innovations, which were called the "Offense of the Seventies." Now, past the midpoint in the decade, many of these things are still being used, but not all by the Chiefs. That great talent aged and Stram was fired.

Another coach who has had success with that type of offense is Tom Landry at Dallas. The Cowboys also line up their fullback in the tight-I, send guys in motion, and run shifts all the time. Our coaches like to play Dallas in the preseason, because they say that Dallas will use everything that we'll face all year. In 1975, Landry dusted off the shotgun for Roger Staubach, and it helped take the Cowboys to the Super Bowl. It's made for Roger, the way he can scramble around back there. We ran the shotgun one time that year, too, and Kansas City's great middle linebacker Willie Lanier threw me for a 15-yard loss, but I can see where we might use it again sometime in the future.

The most successful offense of the 1960s was perhaps the dullest. The Green Bay Packers didn't do anything fancy, they just did it. They won three straight NFL championships and the first two Super Bowls, in 1967 and 1968. They'd run the Green Bay sweep (diagram 10), one of the most devastating plays in football, over and over. They'd send Jim Taylor and Paul Hornung around end behind guards Jerry Kramer and Fuzzy Thurston sometimes 20 times a game. Quarterback Bart Starr was such an accurate passer that he seldom threw interceptions. He'd throw short and intermediate stuff, then fake a running play and get a receiver wide open downfield because everyone respected their run so much.

The Packers were conservative, but did they execute! If they wanted five yards, they'd just go get it. Starr was a very intelligent quarterback and knew how to control the ball. The Pack came out

24

With his running, scrambling, and passing talents, Roger Staubach is made for the shotgun formation. The Cowboys have gone to the shotgun successfully in passing situations.

The Green Bay sweep: Bart Starr (15) has just handed off to fullback Jim Taylor, who is led around end by guards Jerry Kramer (64) and Fuzzy Thurston. They made this basic play one of football's most devastating.

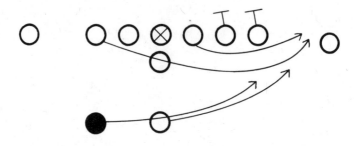

Diagram 10
Green Bay sweep

in a couple of basic formations and ran right at you. They were
worlds apart from, say, the Denver Broncos of today, who use all
kinds of formations, throw the ball often, and run all types of
reverses to wide receivers Jack Dolbin and Rick Upchurch, and
tight end Riley Odoms. About the only thing the Packers did that
was racy at all was the halfback pass with Hornung. They didn't run
it because he was a great passer, though, but to keep people honest
when they'd run that great sweep. The defensive backs couldn't
come up quickly. They had to wait to see if it was a run or pass.

Lombardi had them conditioned, physically and mentally. The
Packers wouldn't beat themselves, and everyone carried out his job.
They were much like the Miami teams that Don Shula coached to a
17-0 record in 1972 and back-to-back Super Bowl wins in 1972 and
1973. The Dolphins would run-run-run with Larry Csonka, Jim
Kiick, and Mercury Morris, and then Bob Griese would throw
mostly short and accurately, run the team with poise, and never get
excited. But the Dolphins had an extra dimension with Paul Warfield, one of the great pass receivers in the game, for the occasional
long bomb.

The 1960s covered most of the career of quarterback Johnny
Unitas, though he's probably most remembered for engineering
that brilliant touchdown drive that beat the New York Giants in
overtime of the 1958 NFL Championship game. To me, Unitas was

This is a double-wing formation: one of the backs stations himself at the end of the line, a yard into the backfield. This is similar to the wing-T offense described in this chapter; but in the wing-T there are two backs behind the quarterback and a wide receiver comes to the wing.

the greatest quarterback who ever played the game. He threw for over 40,000 yards and 250 touchdowns, and that speaks for itself. But he was great at reading defenses and attacking them, though he didn't face the kinds of defenses we face today. None of those great old-time quarterbacks like Bobby Layne, Sammy Baugh, and Otto Graham did. It's a lot tougher these days, but I'm not saying they couldn't play in today's football. If you can throw a ball and have any smarts at all, you can do it. Those guys could play in 1900, now, or in 1990. But they already had man-to-man coverage, the thing we're trying to achieve by using all these formations and shifts.

The American Football League, which prospered and grew enough from 1960 to 1970 to cause a merger with the NFL, was

27

strictly a passing league. There was almost strictly man-to-man coverage. That's why my teammate Willie Brown developed the bump-and-run pass defense. The Oakland Raiders, once Al Davis joined them in 1963, always had the philosophy of throwing the ball. Four Oakland quarterbacks—George Blanda, Daryle Lamonica, Cotton Davidson, and Tom Flores—are ranked in the all-time top 40 for passing yards, and maybe someday there will be five. When Al Davis first came from his assistant coaching job in San Diego to the head coaching spot in Oakland, he already had Davidson and Flores waiting. So he traded for outstanding pass receiver Art Powell and made running back Clem Daniels into one of the most dangerous weapons of his era. Jim Brown was running over people in the NFL for an all-time record 12,312 yards, but Daniels was the Jim Brown of the AFL with combined rushing and receiving yards until a broken leg halted his career in 1967.

Blanda started out with George Halas in Chicago but sat out 1959 over contract disagreements and joined the Houston Oilers in the first year of the AFL. He threw 66 passes in one game, and in one 1963 game he and Flores went at it for four quarters, with Oakland finally winning 52-49 on the only field goal of the game. Blanda had Billy Cannon and Ode Burrell, two sprinters, along with another fine receiver named Charley Hennigan, and he just threw all day.

If Al Davis had taken an NFL coaching job and advocated the running game, he would have traded for a big fullback to go with Daniels, though he eventually got one in Hewritt Dixon, and he would have controlled the ball the way Lombardi's team did. But that wasn't his style and it didn't fit his personnel. Still, the Raiders aren't just a passing team; we're actually pretty balanced and always have been able to run.

Even people who run the wishbone (diagram 11) are beginning to throw more things into their offense. The wishbone, started by former Texas assistant Emory Bellard (who now brings it back with his Texas A&M team to beat old boss Darrell Royal), beat everybody until Notre Dame mirrored it on defense and stopped it in the Cotton Bowl a few years back. Everyone didn't stop using the wishbone, but they realized you must have other things to go with it.

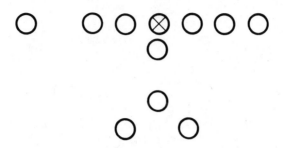

Diagram 11
Wishbone

You've got to take a basic formation that fits your personnel, add a couple of complementary formations around it for variety—and that's your offense. Now it's time to learn the inter-workings of your own system.

# chapter three

AUDIBLE—Quarterback changing play at line of scrimmage.

BACK—A versatile ball carrier-blocker-receiver who lines up behind the quarterback.

BLOCK—An offensive player moving a defensive man to create an opening for a ball carrier.

BLOCKING COMBINATIONS—Teamwork used between blockers against the defense to make a play successful.

CENTER—Middle lineman who snaps ball to quarterback, putting play into motion.

COVERAGE—Strategy by defensive secondary to guard all eligible pass receivers.

END—Block-receiver on the outside of offensive line.

FLARE—Short pass pattern out of the backfield by a running back. Also known as a safety valve.

FORMATION—Type of alignment in which offensive players position themselves at the outset of a play.

FULL HOUSE—All three running backs in the backfield behind the quarterback.

GUARD—Offensive linemen on either side of the center.

HANDOFF—Exchange of ball between two players.

HOLE—Designated area between two blockers through which a running back carries the ball.

HUDDLE—Circular grouping of offense in which the quarterback calls the plays.

LEAD MAN—A running back, acting as a blocker, showing the way through a hole for the ball carrier.

QUARTERBACK—Player responsible for running offense who takes the snap from center to start a play.

SNAP COUNT—Signals called by quarterback while under center to camouflage from defense when ball will be snapped.

TACKLE—Blocker lined up outside the guard and inside the end on offensive line. Also the act of a defensive man taking down a ball carrier.

WEAK SIDE—The side of the offensive line opposite where the tight end lines up. The tight-end side is therefore known as the strong side.

WING—A receiver or back split just outside and behind the line on one side of the offensive formation. One on each side makes a double-wing formation.

# terminology

Before any player can take the field with his team, he must know the language of football. We call it terminology, and it's the difference between sandlot football and the organized brand of ball. Playing on the street, you might tell a guy, "Go long." I've said that a thousand times playing with friends in my home town of Foley, Alabama. When I got to high school football, I learned that you tell a guy to run a certain pattern, like an *up* or a *post* or a *corner*, all of which can be long passes.

When you first join a team, you must learn the particular terminology used there in order to read and understand the plays in that system of offense. When I joined the Raiders in 1968, the first thing Coach Madden talked about to me was terminology. At my first rookie camp they gave me a playbook and we went over that

A player must know his terminology before he goes out onto the field, but with young receivers at a rookie camp here, Coach Tom Flores and the veteran quarterbacks will go over things with the rookies.

several times before we even practiced. Even now when the veterans report to training camp in July of each year, we spend two full days in meetings to go over things. The entire first week is simple, basic football. We go back to the fundamentals, and that starts with terminology.

Without it, a player would be lost. The average fan, listening to Coach Madden and me talking on the sideline, wouldn't know what we're talking about. Playing football without knowing the terminology would be like going to Mexico and attempting to converse with the people without understanding Spanish.

There are certain terms that are universal in football, such as the crackback block, which I've known since I played in high school. But there are differences from team to team in many areas. With the Raiders, when a linebacker rushes the quarterback, we call it a *dog*. Many other teams call this a "blitz."

That's one reason why when a player joins a team after the season has started, he might not play right away even if he's an out-

This is a blitz or a dog, depending on the team's terminology. It's just a linebacker rushing the quarterback in hopes of catching the offense by surprise. This is what happens if it works: no one on the offense picks up the linebacker.

standing player. He must first learn the new system before he can fit easily into it. A player may have been taught something in high school, and may have done the same thing in college and the pros, but the act might be called by an entirely different name on each team.

Terminology is kept simple in high school, but it gets more and more complicated as you go along. I played in the defensive second-ary in high school, and in our zone defense, we had two rota-tions—strong-side and weak-side. In college at Alabama, I also played a little back there and we had a couple more. A pro team might have six or eight of them, with different names such as "Yan-kee" or "Bronco," with options to all of them.

In this chapter, we'll learn some basic terms used in almost all levels of football, and add to them as we progress through the book. Go over the words in the glossary at the beginning of this chapter, and later on in the chapter we'll see how these things are pieced together to run plays from a simple offense and how that differs from our complex offense on the Oakland Raiders.

But, again, remember that some of these things are just examples and may differ from team to team. For instance, even a common term such as a *slant pattern* can be a little bit different depending on the team. In high school, you might run your slant six yards, in college maybe five yards, and in the pros eight yards. Fred Biletnikoff says he hardly ran any patterns until he reached professional football, but the ones he learned when he joined the Raiders were almost totally different from the patterns he did run at Florida State and in high school. Now he runs them better than anyone in football.

Even though our terminology sometimes sounds awfully complex, what it really does is simplify things. Our coaches all talk in these terms—that way everyone understands readily. You just tag things with a certain name. In high school, coaches have to make things very basic because the players are learning football from the beginning and can't be given too many things to worry about at one time. Also, the mental capacity of the players isn't what it will be later on.

Our passing game in high school was just "flanker in, out, or up." In college, I might say, "Pass 50," which meant I would drop straight back, and then I'd tell the receivers to run an *out* or a *comeback*. With the Raiders, it's a lot more complicated, on the one hand, but then again it is easier to do different things, because the offense is so flexible. You can put anyone anywhere you want and have him run any type of pattern.

We label our receivers X, Y and Z. The tight end is Y and the wide receivers are X and Z. Instead of telling them to run a certain pattern, I'll use a number, like 94, and the receiver knows this means to run a *short out*. In the huddle, I can say "X comeback, Y 94, Z 91," and throw in flare action by the back with "7 left," in a second or so. In high school, it would take you too long in the huddle to say all that. All of that may be a little over your head, but it gives you the idea anyway. The more complex your offense is, the more you can manipulate.

My high school and college systems were somewhat similar because my high school coach, Ivan Jones, who coached us to two

This is our huddle, where I call the plays. A player must understand our terminology so that he knows what we are going to do, because there's no time to ask in a game.

state championships and a 29-1 record in three years, was a big advocate of Bear Bryant football. Much of our terminology and strategy, such as the option play, was the same.

Coach Bryant had a television show on Sunday nights, in which he'd go over what happened the day before when Alabama beat Tennessee or whomever, and we always knew that whatever he said on the show, we'd hear from Coach Jones at practice Monday. That made it a bit easier for me when I went to Alabama, because I knew what kind of things I was going to be doing.

We had some interesting terminology at Alabama. We ran a lot of plays from the I-formation, with all of the backs lined up in a single row behind me. If we wanted to be aligned in I-right, I'd call "Gee" in the huddle, and for I-left, I'd say "Haw." Those are the terms you use when driving a pack of mules. If you want them to turn right, you say "Gee;" or left, "Haw." Another formation we put into nautical terms. If we wanted to line up strong to the right, I'd call "Star," for starboard. For left, it was "Port." When you're working with a sophisticated offense, these types of things make it much easier.

For the sake of explaining how an offense works when everyone understands the terminology, and just for fun, let's put together a simple offense and run off some plays. This is basically the type of offense I learned in high school and probably isn't totally unlike the one you'll learn when you begin to play organized football.

First we have to number the holes through which the backs will run. There are gaps between each of the seven offensive linemen (see

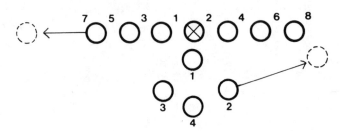

Diagram 12
Hole numbering

36

diagram 12), and the areas outside the ends give us eight holes into which we can run plays. The holes on the right side of the line carry even numbers and the holes to the left are odd-numbered. Between the center and right guard is the two hole, between the right guard and the right tackle is the four hole, between the right tackle and right end is the six hole, and outside the end is the eight hole. To the left, counting from the center out, it's just the same, only the numbers are odd—one, three, five, seven.

As you can see in the diagram, the quarterback is given the number one, the right halfback number two, the left halfback number three and the fullback number four. This numbering system is not universal, but it is very popular. I've been fortunate that it's been the same on all three teams I've played for—at Foley High, Alabama, and Oakland, except that the Raiders don't number the backs. Some coaches number their holes from one through eight left-to-right, while others do it right-to-left.

Now, if we call a 47 from this offense, it's just the number-four back—the fullback—carrying the ball to the seven hole, in a sweep around left end. If a 36 is called, the left halfback runs an off-tackle play to the right side. The blocking on these plays is strictly man-on-man, meaning the linemen block the opponent in front of them and the lead man blocks the first opponent he sees. Later, it gets more complicated, as you'll see. If we want to run a straight dive play, it's a 24 for the right halfback and a 33 for the left halfback. Every play is predetermined and there are no options in the middle of a play, but many high schools have gone to the triple-option, in which the quarterback makes split-second play changes. An experienced high school quarterback may also learn to call simple audibles, which are also known as automatics or check-offs.

Though we're lined up in the basic full-house backfield in the diagram, our bread-and-butter formation is the wing-T, with either the right or left halfback lined up just outside and behind the tight end on his side. The tight ends also may split out a few yards to facilitate easier release on passing downs. These adjustments are shown in diagram 12 by the arrows and the 12th and 13th players shown in dotted lines.

Say we're faced with a third-down play, with two yards to go for

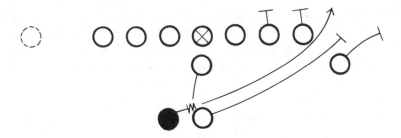

Diagram 13
Wing right 36

a first down. In the huddle, our quarterback picks a solid short-yardage play. He'll call it by saying, "Wing right, 36, on two." *Wing right* is the formation, *36* is the play (three back into the six hole), and *two* signifies the count on which the center will snap the ball to the quarterback, starting the play (see diagram 13). The right halfback sets up out behind the right end, because we are in "Wing Right." The quarterback is under the center, calling his signals, "Ready, set, hut-one, hut-two!" On the count of two, everyone on the offensive team springs into action at once. The line charges at the defensive linemen and drives them backward. The fullback leads the halfback into the hole and blocks the first man he sees, perhaps a linebacker. The quarterback makes a half-spin to his left and hands the ball off to the left halfback, who feels for the ball instead of looking for it. He must keep his head up and look for the hole his blockers have bored in the defense. There it is, and our man zips through it for a four-yard gain and a first down. As simple as that play is, you couldn't run it unless you knew our terminology.

That's a very basic play, undoubtedly used by every offense in America, each with its own peculiarities. We ran the same play at Alabama and called it similarly; but with the Raiders, our "36" becomes something else again. First of all, we have a different formation. We have two wide receivers and one tight end, though if we

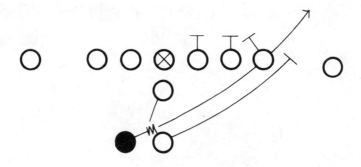

Diagram 14
16 Bob-tray-O

run that off-tackle play in a short-yardage situation, chances are we will have two, or even three, tight ends in the game for added blocking power.

Diagram 13 showed you how we ran our 36, and diagram 14 is the way it looks with the Raiders. Instead of "Wing Right," we call if *far right*, meaning the tight end is on the right side, making it the strong side of the formation, and the halfback is in the farthest backfield position from the tight end.

Instead of "36," we call it "16 Bob-Tray-O." We don't number our backs, as I said earlier, but we run series of plays. For instance, on our 40 series, we run our traps with the guards pulling, and our 60 series is run to the weak-side tackle. Our strong-side tackle plays are teen numbers, such as this 16. If we ran it to the other side, it would be 17, behind All-Pro tackle Art Shell. When we run it to the right, as in this case, it's 16, with the Bob-Tray-O signifying the blocking combinations. A Bob block is the fullback (say Marv Hubbard) leading the halfback (probably Clarence Davis) and blocking the man on the end of the line of scrimmage. A Tray block is the tight end and tackle John Vella double-teaming the defensive end.

Again, it's the same play we ran out of our wing-T offense, but with more advanced trappings. However, when I call it in the huddle, everyone knows what I'm talking about because we're working

39

Here's our Wing right 36 play, or as the Raiders call it, "Strong right, 16-Bob-tray-O." Halfback Harold Hart is running behind fullback Marv Hubbard into the six hole, between the tight end and the tackle.

on the same wavelength. This is one of our big short-yardage plays, and it's probably as old as football itself. There are many plays, such as this, that are run from the peewee leagues right on through the pros, but each team calls and runs them its own special way. It's part of a team's personality.

Every team has a play or series of plays that it makes a living on.

In other words, these plays are used often, but if you execute them well enough, other teams can't stop you. The Green Bay teams of Vince Lombardi made the Packer sweep famous, and at USC, John McKay made the off-tackle blast a household word with tailbacks such as O. J. Simpson, Mike Garrett, Clarence Davis, Anthony Davis, and Ricky Bell. The Raiders are known for their weak-side running game, behind Shell and guard Gene Upshaw, another All-Pro. Other teams have these plays, and may run and call them nearly the same, but that's when the importance of terminology ends. When you get out on the field, it all comes down to outdoing the other guy, because you both should know what you're doing. But this is definitely a thinking man's game.

Before we get out of terminology and get on to how you use it once everything is straight in your mind, here are some more interesting bits of things I've picked up over the years and exactly what they mean, in case you ever hear them.

Many teams use colors in their terminology. Our three-tight-end offense is called "Tight Blue." When we see a three-lineman, four-linebacker defense, we call it "Orange." The Miami Dolphins made it famous as their "53 Defense," but the Raiders used it way back in 1967 when defensive tackle Tom Keating was injured. You see the 3-4 defense all the time now, but it's a relatively new thing in the pros. We saw a lot of it in college, and it's basically the same "Okie Defense" that Bud Wilkinson built a powerhouse around at Oklahoma more than 20 years ago.

The New York Jets use colors to call audibles. Many times I've heard Joe Namath call his signals, "Green, 99, hut-one, hut-two." Say red is the live color for the day; if the first thing Namath says at the line of scrimmage is "Red," then the play he called in the huddle is off and the next thing he says is the new play. If Joe says, "Green," or any other color, the original play is on. We do it a little differently, with numbers. If I call, "69, boom, man, cloud" in the huddle, and the first thing I say at the line is "69," then that play is off and something else is coming. That alerts everybody that I've spotted something in the defense and I don't want to run that play, or maybe I prefer another one. *Boom* means the halfback blocks a linebacker. *Man* is man-to-man blocking in the line, and *Cloud* tells

41

the tight end to block the cornerback. Again, this is just to give you an idea of how things are done. It gets even more complicated, because the linemen can change the blocking combinations themselves at the line of scrimmage—but we won't get into that. You don't have to concern yourself with these things, just concentrate on the basic terminology and formations you have to work with.

Defensive calls are interesting, especially when you're a quarterback and have to learn to recognize instantly what the other team is conjuring up to stop you. "Cloud" and "sky" are support calls between a cornerback and safety to help out against the run. Safety George Atkinson of the Raiders might yell "sky" to cornerback Skip Thomas. That means if Atkinson reads a sweep to their side, he's forcing right now, while Thomas drops off in case it's a fake and the pass is coming. If Atkinson calls "Cloud," Thomas comes up and George drops back.

Our defensive backfield has eight basic coverages, all with several options. They number them one through eight and make them readily recognizable with code words. Coverage one is "Ollie," after Coach Ollie Spencer. Coverage four is "Fox," six is "Sam," and eight is "Ed." When we send in a fifth defensive back, we call him "the Pirate." Defensive teams are always yelling out different things, such as the names of towns. They yell out "Cincinnati," or something, but I just figure that much of that stuff is dummy calls that they make to confuse you. I try not to listen.

Blitzes and dogs—linebackers rushing the quarterback, as I explained earlier—can be kind of funny. If both outside linebackers are coming, we call it a "Red Dog." The middle linebacker coming on a blitz is a "Monster." "Bronco" is a weak-side dog, and if all the linebackers are coming, we call it a "Mad Tiger." But the best one is when a safety comes from a strange position. That's a "Blue Lulu."

But once more, let me emphasize that these aren't universal terms. Some of them are used by some teams, but other clubs might call the same thing by a completely different name. For example, I always knew the middle linebacker as "the Mike." But then one year at the Pro Bowl, I heard someone from another team refer to him as "the Mac." In our terminology, "the Mac" is a defensive lineman who positions himself in front of the center—on his nose, as we say.

Now that you know why terminology is used and understand a little bit of it yourself, you're ready to go out and line up—but on the practice field first.

# chapter four

No matter how good a team you have, if you're not ready to play when you go out on the field, there's a good chance you may get beat. A player must be prepared individually as much as the entire team must be, because if that one guy makes one or two mistakes, those mistakes may cause breakdowns that lose the game even if everyone else is playing up to capabilities.

There are two types of basic preparation—physical and mental. First, your body has to be in shape, and that begins long before you go out to play a game. We'll get into off-season conditioning, training camp programs, and things you do during the season to maintain the shape you've built up. These are vitally important, because you cannot take advantage of your skills if your body is not in top condition.

# preparation

The other type of preparation is mental, and it's equally important. You can't go all out, give 110 percent, if you're not quite sure or don't know what you're doing. There are a couple of aspects to mental readiness. One is knowing the game plan, the plays and tactics your team plans to use against an opponent. The other part is putting everything else out of your mind and concentrating the entire way on the task at hand.

Both types of preparation are equally important. You can't get by with just one or the other. I've taken pride throughout my career on being mentally ready to compete. I honestly believe that I've been ready to play every time I've gone out on the field, even though my play may not have shown it at times. The only times I haven't been totally prepared physically have been because of injuries.

You must be ready to play every time you go out on the field, or chances are that you'll lose. I honestly believe that I've been mentally prepared every time I've gone out to play. Here George Blanda and I come out of the tunnel before a game.

You can't rely on what happened in the past—the last time you played a certain team, for example. If you beat them before, you have to be ready to go out and do it again the next time you play them. You can't figure that, just because you won last week and played pretty well, you're just going to go out on the field and do it again.

46

I can use the 1974 playoffs as an excellent example of being prepared one week and not being ready the next. In the first round against Miami, the two-time Super Bowl champion, we were mentally and physically prepared to play. Even though they ran the opening kickoff back for a touchdown, and were ahead most of the game, we came back and won in the final minute on a TD pass I threw to Clarence Davis. Coming from behind is a trait the Raiders have had over the years, and we'll talk about that later in this chapter.

We had to play Pittsburgh the next week in the American Football League Championship Game, but all that next week everyone was still talking about the Miami game and saying that since the Raiders won that game they should be on their way to the Super Bowl. We honestly tried to get ready for the Steelers, and going into the game I felt that we were. But looking back on it now, I can see that we weren't, possibly because of the emotion left over from the Miami game. But it was a subconscious thing and we couldn't recognize it then. I'm not saying that's the reason we lost, because the Steelers played well and certainly had a lot to do with it, but our not being prepared was a factor in our losing.

As I said before, preparation begins long before you ever take the practice field. In pro football, it's become a full-time job to stay in shape. You can't afford to do nothing for the rest of the year, because everyone else is working to be ready. We play the game six months of the year, beginning with training camp in July and running through the playoffs in December and January. So you can't get totally out of shape, because it comes around again too soon. But you can't afford to go to camp having done nothing during the off season, because there isn't enough time to get into shape from step one. When you've stayed in decent shape, your conditioning comes much easier.

I'm not saying that you should play football every day for 12 months a year. You should just keep active doing something. You can play basketball, tennis, golf, handball, or participate in any other type of physical activity. You can't abandon activity completely. Some guys never stop working out. When All-Pro tackle Bob Brown was with the Raiders, he lifted weights almost every day

It can be beneficial for a quarterback to work out informally with his receivers and backs during the off season. Here I'm with Clarence Davis at the Raider practice field in Oakland just before camp.

48

of the year, in and out of football season, and I'm sure he still does. Fred Biletnikoff runs an awful lot and plays basketball and golf during the off season. Cliff Branch runs on the pro track tour and I'm sure the conditioning to stay in shape for that is tough. Most of our linemen and linebackers lift weights.

My off season consists mostly of lifting weights and maybe swimming; I can't do the things I'd like to because my knees are bad. I like to play basketball; I averaged 29 points a game in high school, but I can't play at all. I used to play for the Raiders' off-season basketball team, but the last time I did was three or four years ago. I just try to watch my weight, even though I do play a little tennis. But I don't dive after any balls or go from sideline to sideline. I'd like to try snow skiing and some other things, but it's too risky.

When I went to high school, it wasn't any problem keeping in shape after football because I went right into basketball, then into baseball, and played baseball all summer long right back into football. I know that kids don't do that as much any more, but it was expected then, and I enjoyed playing all the sports. In high school you have gym class and other things to keep you active, but once you get into college you have to find things after football is over in order to keep in decent shape.

When you work out for football on your own, just practice the things you'll be doing during the season. If you are a lineman, get in your stance and fire out on the different blocking assignments you may have. Or do the drills you use during the season. There isn't too much else you can do, except your running and weight training.

Quarterbacks should attempt to work out together with their receivers and backs, running the pass patterns and plays they'll be using when the season starts. It will help just to get familiar with each other's moves. Working alone, quarterbacks can go over the footwork they use for different plays. You can work on your different drops on pass plays, going right from the snap from center to your follow-through.

If you want to build up your passing arm, the best thing to do is throw the ball as much as you can. Just play catch. But I also believe that a quarterback can build himself up by lifting weights. I know a lot of coaches will disagree with me there. They don't like to

If a quarterback wants to strengthen his throwing arm and improve his accuracy, the best thing is to just throw the ball all the time. That's before, during, and after practice—and even on your spare time.

have their quarterbacks lifting because it tends to tighten up their arm and shoulder muscles. I'm not saying you should lift and then go out and practice. Lift after practice and then go home and sleep on it, or lift during the off season to build up your throwing arm.

I didn't do much weight lifting in high school and college because I didn't feel I needed it. My arm was strong enough then and I felt that, at 180 or so pounds, I was big enough. But when I came to the Raiders, I saw that I would need a stronger and quicker arm. I also realized that I would be playing against bigger defensive linemen, so I built up my upper body in order to absorb some of the shots that a quarterback always takes.

Actually, it's kind of funny how I got involved in weight lifting. When I came to Oakland, I began hanging around with guys like

I believe a quarterback should strengthen his upper body—not only to improve his throwing arm but in order to take shots like this, which he's going to take from defensive linemen who weigh up to 300 pounds.

Tony Cline, our defensive end, and Dan Conners, then our middle linebacker. They lifted weights often, so I was exposed to it and started doing it myself. It really helped me, because I gained 10 pounds each year for the first four seasons I was with the Raiders, until I weighed 220. That might be too much, but it's easy for me to cut down five or so pounds. Some guys don't especially like to lift weights; I don't think Tony does, for instance, but I enjoyed it right away. I think I lifted every day during one off season, but they say that's not good for you, that you should lift every other day. But I really felt I was doing myself some good, so I did it. I got to where I could bench press 300 pounds, and that's quite a bit for a quarterback. But I wasn't trying to see how much I could lift, it's just that I lifted so much that I progressed to that point.

I'm a real advocate of weight lifting for football players, even young football players. It definitely can help you. But don't just go out and start lifting weights indiscriminately. Consult with a coach

After practice at training camp, the Raiders head for their outside weight-lifting area. I'm a real advocate of weight training, even for a quarterback, because it can improve you as a player.

or with someone else who can tell you which parts of your body you need to work on. And map out a workout program. A strong guy is going to overpower a weak guy, and a fast guy is going to beat a slow guy in football, but you can improve yourself in those areas. Weight lifting is a way you can do that.

Weight training has become a big part of football. Our linemen lift three times a week during the season, but they do it after practice. You can't follow a heavy weight-training program during the season because you have to save your strength for the games each week. That's important, because even a 10-game season can seem like an eternity. We play six preseason games and 14 league games just to get to the playoffs. So the time to build yourself up is the off season, or training camp. During the season, whatever work you do is done to keep up your level of conditioning.

All of this other training brings you into spring practice and preseason drills—training camp, for us. The Raiders spend six weeks in Santa Rosa, a small town 60 miles north of Oakland. It's nothing but football all day long. There's nothing else to do and no time to do it. We have two practices and at least one meeting every day. It's a time when you must concentrate 100 percent on football. This is your preparation for the season and it's important that you get the most out of it.

The conditioning you get in training camp is a base that will carry you through the long grind of the season. Once the season starts, there isn't time to worry about conditioning because all of your time is spent getting ready for the game that week. Training camp is the formal beginning of your preparation for the season. Everything you did during the off season, though it also was important, was just to get ready for this.

Preseason practice is the start of your physical and mental preparation for the season. Though you've kept in pretty decent shape during the off season, being in shape to play a season of football is an entirely different matter. Many guys come to camp feeling that they're really in good shape, only to discover differently on the very first day. You concentrate on many drills that will help get you into shape; in addition, all the work you do in two practices a day going over the things you'll be doing all season helps you build up the condition of your body.

Mentally, this is important to you because it gets you back into a football frame of mind. It's mental conditioning. Not only do you relearn the offense from the ground up, but you begin to build an attitude and a camaraderie on your team that is necessary to a winning football team.

Before you begin practicing, there are still more critical things you must be concerned with. The first is equipment. Football can be a dangerous game, even with all the modern equipment and aids we have. People are going to get hurt. It's the nature of the game. That's why it's necessary that you be equipped properly when you take the field. Proper equipment and maintenance of this equipment keeps injuries to the bare minimum.

I believe that all organized football programs do a good job of furnishing equipment. They purchase helmets and pads that are solidly constructed. Some of them get into trouble when the equipment doesn't fit properly. This happens when, say, a ninth-grader comes in on his first day and gets a helmet that is too big. All these big juniors and seniors are standing around and the younger guy isn't going to say, "Give me another helmet, Coach, this one is too big."

I'm not saying this happens everywhere, but I've seen it take place. You must make sure that your shoes fit properly; that you have knee pads, thigh pads, hip pads, shoulder pads, and a helmet; and that all of them are adjusted so they fit you the way they are meant to. Your pants and jersey must be snug enough to keep your pads from bouncing around, yet loose enough so as not to inhibit your movement. I've seen young guys come out to practice with their thigh pads hanging down below their knees. You just can't play normally this way.

When you come out to practice or play, even if you're just working out by yourself, the most important thing is to make sure you are warmed up before starting hard work. This is important in anything you do—baseball, golf, tennis, basketball, or any other physical activity. You must make your muscles looser than normal before you start. I don't walk out onto the field and start throwing the ball as hard as I can. I do it gradually. In fact, I don't even throw for the first 15 or 20 minutes.

In all organized programs, the coaches have good warm-up programs to get you ready. It's very easy to pull muscles or hurt yourself if you're not completely loose.

With the Raiders, we break off into groups for our exercise period at the start of practice. The offensive line, defensive line, linebackers, defensive backs, and running backs break off into

In practice, especially at training camp, you do things over and over again. But it's part of your mental preparation to be ready for this and to keep going full blast. Here I am with Jess Phillips in a passing drill.

separate groups, and in my group it's the quarterbacks and receivers. We form a circle and go through various stretching and loosening drills, plus sit-ups and other exercises to start with. Then the receivers run their pass patterns at half speed and the quarterbacks—such as George Blanda, David Humm, and myself—start out by lobbing the ball and gradually working up to full strength.

After the first few days, practice may be the worst part of football. There aren't a lot of players who are in love with it. But that's part of your mental preparation. You know it's going to be like that and you must be ready to deal with it. Practice is nothing but repetition. You run the same plays over and over and over. That's the best way to learn something so well that it becomes second nature. Sure, it becomes boring at times, but you must do it because it's going to help you later on. Fred Biletnikoff, Cliff Branch, and Mike Siani run the same patterns over and over, but pretty soon I get to know where they are going, to the exact spot. That will help us in game situations.

Soon, you do your job without even thinking. It becomes instinct. If you want to learn to hit the curve ball, you have someone throw it to you over and over until you can hit it in your sleep. You get sick and tired of doing it in practice, but that makes it so much easier when you get into a game. When you run a play and it works, you can understand why you practiced it so much. You get a big feeling of accomplishment knowing the effort paid off.

I've always heard that when you get tired late in practice, that's when it's doing you the most good. I know coaches preach this to their players. I believe it, up to a point. If you are able to keep going when you get tired and accomplish the things you are supposed to, then it's a big plus. However, there's a fine line: when you reach a point where you're so tired that it affects your efficiency, you're not getting much good from it. I don't feel that it does you good just to be "out there." In fact, if a player is basically just "out there," it can hurt him, because he may get into bad habits.

But I definitely believe in hard work. Playing with a team like the Raiders, I know that it can pay off. We have a reputation of sometimes wearing other teams down during the second half, in addition to having a history of coming from behind to last-minute victories.

Those aren't miracles, they are partly due to conditioning and hard work; but you can't depend on doing that all the time.

We've had some great ones, such as the famous "Heidi Game" and that playoff triumph over Miami, but there have been many others. I believe there are a couple of reasons for our success in that type of situation, the kind every team finds itself in from time to time no matter how good it is. First of all, we have the personnel to do those things. When you come from behind, you almost always have to do it with passing. We have exceptional receivers and our offensive line gives me all the time I need with superb pass blocking. I always feel we can win with these outstanding players. And we never believe we're beaten.

But I think that our conditioning has much to do with it. We stay in training camp longer than any other team in pro football and also have two-a-day workouts more than other teams. I'm not saying we're in better shape than all the other teams, but I don't think any team is better conditioned than we are. We're still going strong at the end of the half, at the end of the game, in overtime if we go that far, and at the end of the season.

Our practices are normally about two hours long, sometimes a little more and occasionally somewhat less. We start out, as I pointed out before, with each unit working by itself. Gradually, we piece our team together as practice wears on. We might have the receivers go against the coverage of our defensive backs, then add the linebackers and bring the running backs in. It helps our offense to go against guys like Otis Sistrunk, Tony Cline, Phil Villapiano, Willie Brown, Jack Tatum, and all our outstanding defensive players during practice. If you are an offensive player, you should help your defense all you can, and vice versa, on the practice field. Even though there is a natural rivalry between such units on the same team, when you get out there for a game, you're all on the same side.

By the end of practice, we get together for team work. That's the full offense going against the full defense. This is where you put together everything you've learned, and this is the situation most like game action that you can have during practice. We don't scrimmage very often, but we have many live drills without tack-

We run strides after practice, not sprints. These 100-yard runs are not to get you into shape but to keep you there. We run in groups by position, and here I am a few years ago with George Blanda and Daryle Lamonica.

ling—even though we get surprise tackles from time to time—that serve much the same purpose.

Practice during training camp differs greatly from what you'll be doing during the season. Even the pros go back to the basics, the fundamentals, during camp. We start right from the beginning like

58

everyone else. You go over everything that you might try during the season. Once the regular season comes, you don't have time for that. You go over a different game plan every week and practice that until you know and understand all the assignments for that week. You learn about the other team and what it is likely to do against you. If we're playing our longtime rivals, the Kansas City Chiefs, we'll watch our past films of the Chiefs plus the games they've played so far that year. When there is a game approaching, you must have tunnel-vision. You can't afford to let anything else enter your mind.

At the end of almost every practice, Coach Madden has us run 100 yards perhaps five times. But these are not the sprints that many teams run at the conclusion of practice. We call them "strides." You don't run them full speed, just at a fast enough speed that you feel you're getting some good from it. Strides are not meant to get you into shape, they are to keep you there. They help you stay in good condition throughout the season.

Following our formal practice, we have a specialty period. During this time, I work with George Blanda and center Dave Dalby, though for most of my career it was the great Jim Otto, on our field goals and extra points. On our other practice field, Ray Guy and the punt and kickoff teams work on their responsibilities. But it's not just a time for special teams. Quarterbacks and receivers or backs will stay after practice to work on pass routes, and may even work one-on-one against defensive backs. Tight ends may work against linebackers, while offensive linemen work on techniques with defensive linemen on a man-against-man basis. These post-practice drills can be as important as many of the things you do during the regular workout. This is the way second-stringers improve themselves. It's much easier to do these things once the season starts, because when training camp finishes, we go down to one practice a day and it's much less strenuous. But you see some of this extra work even in camp.

All of these types of preparation are important, but the most critical type to a football player comes from within himself. Some people go out for football and think, "I'm going to try my best to make the team," or you can say to yourself, "I'm going to be the best player I can be and I'm going to make all-conference." Your attitude is very important to the way you are going to play. You have to believe your team is going to win. When you go out to play a game, you have to think you're going to do your best, but you can take that one step further and say, "We're going to knock the other team around." To me, that's the only attitude you can take in sports. You have to know that you're going to be good, even if you must work your tail off to get there. You can't think, "I'm not a very good player, not as good as this guy is, but maybe I'll make the team," or, "I'll be second string."

You have to believe you're going to make it, and even if you're not starting, you have to believe you are as good as the guy who's playing in front of you. Monte Johnson, who plays middle line-backer for us in Oakland, never started a game throughout college at Nebraska nor during his first two years with the Raiders, but I know he always believed he was good enough to start.

I've been second-string three times in my football career, and each time I thought I was better than the guy in front of me. I may not have been, looking back on it now, but there was no way you could have convinced me of it at that time. When I came to the Raiders, Daryle Lamonica had just taken them to the Super Bowl. But there was no doubt in my mind that I was as good as he was, even though 40 or so other people with the Raiders didn't think so. But you couldn't tell me that or ever hear me admit it.

At Alabama, I played behind Steve Sloan as a sophomore. He's now the coach at Texas Tech and was an excellent quarterback. He played most of the time and led us to the Orange Bowl, but I played when he was hurt or if our offense wasn't going well. I didn't beat him out, but I thought I was better. Coach Bryant didn't, though, and he's about the greatest coach around.

High school was the same way. When I was a sophomore, I played behind a guy named Lester Smith. He was a good player, played junior college football, and now coaches the high school team in Foley. It was kind of the same thing then, though when you're a sophomore in high school, you kind of figure that if there's a senior quarterback, he's going to start. But inside, I thought I was as good or better than Lester.

But he was two years older than me, bigger, stronger, and I can say it now, probably better. When you're a competitor—something that I pride in myself—it's difficult to sit and wait on the bench. I spent five years waiting around in Oakland, and it nearly killed me. But, in retrospect, I can understand it now. Still, if I had to do it all over again, I could never accept it in my mind. That's the attitude it takes. You can talk to anyone who's been successful at almost anything in life, and I'll bet he or she has that type of mental attitude.

But, going back to the beginning of the chapter, you can't get by just with the mental aspect. You must be prepared to play both physically and mentally. Your mental attitude can affect your physical performance, and vice versa. If you are in a good frame of mind, you can do things confidently and naturally. When you are in your best physical condition, you know it and it gives you a positive mental attitude. That, I've found, can be an almost unbeatable combination on the football field.

# chapter five

Practically every move you make on the football field should be done in a certain way, though in some cases there is more than one correct way, depending on who teaches it to you. These methods are commonly known as techniques. A person with less athletic talent or less strength or less speed can often beat a player with more natural ability by using the correct techniques. There are times when you won't be able to use your techniques exactly the way they are meant to be used because you can't control what your opponent will do; but football is a game of spontaneity and you must react accordingly.

There is a certain way to position yourself for every move—where your head should be, how much your feet should be spread, which way you should be looking, and so on. But the main

# techniques

thing to remember about everything you do is that you should be as balanced as possible when doing anything—running, blocking, passing, or receiving. When you are in balance, you can best take advantage of your physical abilities. We will go over some techniques for each offensive position, and you'll notice that in each case balance is most important. This is also known as body control. A player may knock you off balance slightly, but you can still make the play if you maintain body control.

We'll start out with the quarterback position because naturally that's the one I know best, and progress through the whole offense. I don't want to make it seem that I consider myself an expert on all positions, but as the quarterback, it's part of my job to know an awful lot about the total offensive picture. Since the quarterback must relate to all offensive positions, I feel that my exposure to them gives me some basic knowledge of all of them.

QUARTERBACK—Even some people who watch football an awful lot take for granted the center snap, but it's vital to the success of a play because that's where it all starts. You must work with your center on the snap just like anything else until it's second nature. Even though I'm left-handed, I hold my hands just like a right-hander, with the right hand on top. The fingers are spread and the hands come together right at the base of the wrists. The right hand is placed under the center's rump and the hands are held firm, but not rigid, or the ball will bounce off. The left hand traps the ball when the center snaps it back. The quarterback should be far enough under the center so that the ball reaches him, but not so far that it's difficult to pull away after the snap. All centers are different because each has a different height and build, so you must work with all of your centers to be familiar with them. The quarterback should have his feet about shoulder-width apart, his head up in order to see downfield, and his back straight. This is a good, balanced position. The most important thing is to feel comfortable.

The quarterback's turns are also important, because if he goes the wrong way, it winds up as a broken play that can kill a series and a drive. It's important on each play to remember which foot you are going to pick up and which one you will plant, put your weight on, and push off with. This is something you learn naturally with the repetition of practicing each play many times.

On the drop-back pass, I push off with my right foot, while right-handers push off with their left. Whichever one you use, drive off that foot to give you a quick push back because a play develops rapidly and you have only so long to get the pass off. After you push off, cross over your feet left-right-left-right until you are 10 yards—or whatever distance your coach teaches you—behind the line of scrimmage. You keep your head and eyes facing downfield all during your drop, and hold the ball high so you can be ready to get the pass off as quickly as necessary. When you reach the end of your drop, plant your back foot and leave your feet about shoulder-width apart in a comfortable passing stance. Everyone has his own

## THE DROP-BACK PASS

The quarterback's hands are held together at the base of the wrist on the center snap, with the fingers spread. The hands are held under the rump of the center, who fires out as he snaps the ball.

As a left-hander, I push off into my drop with the right foot; a right-hander pushes off with his left foot. Take a good grip of the ball in case you take a hit right away.

Cross your feet over, left-right-left-right-left, in your drop, sliding your fingers around the ball until they are on the laces and you are ready to throw the ball quickly if you get pressure.

Keep your eyes downfield on the defense and your receivers at all times, not letting the action in the line distract you.

When you reach the end of your drop, plant your back foot—the left one in my case, the right one for right-handers—and keep the ball up in a passing position.

When you throw the ball, keep it up high; don't hitch and drop it down to your waist for extra power, because it can throw off your accuracy. Keep your eye on the receiver and step in the direction of the receiver as you release the ball.

70

Release the ball from a high point in your passing arc; follow through with your arm, legs, and body after you throw the ball.

passing style, but there are basic techniques to perform. Always try to step in the direction in which you are throwing. Throw the ball overhand, not sidearm or three-quarters. This may not be possible because of onrushing linemen and other circumstances, but attempt to release the ball from a high point. Don't forget to follow through. If you are forced to scramble, and you see a man open, get the ball there the best way you can; there's no time to concern yourself with form when you scramble. When I get tired, I find myself throwing the ball sidearm and doing other things incorrectly. That's the time you must strive to do it right. I don't consider myself a picture passer like Johnny Unitas or Bart Starr, but there aren't too many like that. The main thing is the end result, a completion. Bobby Layne wasn't a picture passer, nor was Billy Kilmer, but they got the job done. The same principles hold true on pitchouts. Stay on balance, look at the target, and follow through. Try not to hurry, though sometimes you are forced into it. If you throw one away, forget it, just as you must do with interceptions and fumbles. They happen to everybody, and you can't let them affect your game.

RUNNING BACK—This position, more than any other, probably requires a player with natural talent. Running with the football, for the most part, is raw ability and instinct, the kind of thing you can't teach. Either a guy can do it or he can't. But there are little fine points, such as switching the ball from one hand to the other in traffic and protecting the ball in pileups, that a back can learn. When running with the football through the line, a back should cover it with both arms to prevent it from being knocked out by one of the many collisions he's going to have. When running in the open field, he should cradle the ball firmly in one arm, one point in the cup of his hand and the other tip in the crook of his elbow.

A back should take a three-point stance that enables him to go forward, right, or left with equal quickness because he must be able to get into a play or a pattern in any of these directions. His weight should be distributed evenly on both feet so that he can do this, and he may have his weight slightly forward on the balls of his feet because he rarely, if ever, goes backward. The back should line up square to the line of scrimmage every time—and use exactly the

This is the way we hand off. The running back raises the arm closest to the quarterback and stretches the far arm across his middle with the palm and forearm up. The quarterback places the ball on the forearm, looking it all the way in. The back here is fullback Hewritt Dixon in training camp, 1971.

same stance every time—because it can be very easy to give away the play. You can't lean or cheat to the left if the play is going that way, because a smart defensive man will pick that up and move that way to stop the play. Even if your head is cocked the way you're going, or if your eyes are looking at the hole where you will be running, it can give the defense a clue to what you're up to. Find a comfortable stance from which you can do everything you must, and use it each time.

There are two styles of taking a handoff from the quarterback, but I believe one is decidedly better than the other. The best way is to put the arm away from the quarterback across your midsection with the palm up. The hand closest to the quarterback is pointed to the opposite arm's bend in the elbow, and the elbow nearest the quarterback is held as high as possible. This gives the quarterback a very large, open target and he simply places the ball on the lower forearm. Then the back closes both arms around the ball. Quarterbacks should take notice of this, because the quarterback must make sure he gets close enough to the back going by or there is a tendency to toss the ball. Also, *look* the ball onto the back's forearm, because if you don't it's easy to push the ball through his arms or leave it short on his hip. Both players should be well-balanced at the point of handoff.

Some teams teach their backs to just hold their hands down and close together in sort of a breadbasket style. I know that O. J. Simpson does it that way in Buffalo. But the other way seems much safer to me. It would seem that the breadbasket leaves much more open room, and might be more prone to missed handoffs. But do it the way your coach *teaches* you.

RECEIVERS—Wide receivers take more of a track stance than running backs, because they must get downfield quickly. All of the weight must be forward because it's important that the receiver gets into his pattern right at the snap of the ball. Some receivers like the traditional three-point stance, while others prefer to stand straight up with one leg canted back (with which to push off). It doesn't matter which one you use, just so you're comfortable. I've watched Fred Biletnikoff so much, talked with him, and one thing that he says over and over is that a receiver must always have his feet under him. Freddie has such great body control that he can make exacting cuts and is always under control. He sometimes seems to be gliding along when really he's running quite rapidly. It's difficult to make your cuts when you are running full speed, so take a little bit off and you'll find yourself running better patterns.

When catching the ball—and I'm sure you've heard this hundreds of times already—look the ball into your hands. It's easy to turn your head away and start running before the ball is all the way into your hands. After you catch it, bring it in to your body and protect it, because more than likely you're going to get hit. The Raiders teach a slightly different technique for catching balls from the waist

Here is Fred Bi-
letnikoff, show-
ing how our re-
ceivers catch
balls above the
waist. The arms
are extended
with the thumbs
pointed in, so
the receiver
can catch the
ball at the far-
thest possible
point away from
his body.

up when facing the quarterback. Extend your arms to full length and exactly parallel to the flight of the ball. Keep your hands together, with the thumbs in. Others teach you to catch the ball with the thumbs out and your hands in front of your chest. But our coaches feel that with your arms at full length, you'll catch the ball split seconds sooner, and this may make the difference in holding it when hit by a defender. Or, if there is a defender right with you fighting you for the ball, you should reach it before he does.

Our coaches teach receivers not to dive for the ball on long passes that are slightly overthrown. When you leave your feet, you lose all of your momentum, momentum that might carry you to the ball. Our receivers run through the ball, figuring that if they don't reach the ball that way, they wouldn't have reached it by diving. But the main thing with catching any pass is concentration. When the ball is in the air, you watch it and don't think of anything else. That's as important as good hands. Freddie is so good that he doesn't even need two hands. He's caught touchdowns with one hand and has become so adept at it that all of our receivers practice catching the ball with just one hand for those times when you can't get to the ball with two, or if a defender grabs your other one.

LINEMEN—The techniques used in the offensive line are just about the same from one position to the next, including tight end, which uses some of the techniques of a lineman and some of a pass receiver. The basic lineman's stance is, once again, the three-point stance, with feet spread about shoulder-width apart and slightly staggered, with the weight evenly distributed between the fingers and the two feet. You must be able to power straight ahead or pull both right and left. But your head should be straight up and aimed at the defensive lineman's chin. This doesn't mean that you'll always be blocking him head-on, but you must align yourself this way every time in order not to give your move away. The left guard may be pulling to the right, but he can't lean that way, because the defender will read it. You must look the same every time. You can't drop your back foot farther back on pass plays to set up more easily for pass blocking, because it will tip off the play. If a defensive lineman sees that you have the weight back on your heels, he'll know that either you are going to pull or pass block. If he sees that you have all of your weight forward on your fingers, he'll know that you are planning to drive straight out on him. Therefore, you must have an evenly balanced stance on both running and passing plays.

The basic block of football is the drive block, whether you are a lineman, a tight end, or a running back. You fire out on the defensive man, driving off your back foot and exploding into the defender's body while staying low. Once you hit him a good lick, you can't stop, but must continue to drive him backward and sustain the block. But your explosion must be under control, because if your body gets ahead of your feet, you become extended and lose your power, so it becomes easy for the defensive man to push you to the ground. Then he can go around you and make the play. You can't lunge; you must drive and pull your legs up underneath you and block the man backward, staying with him. The ideal is to knock the man down, but you can't always do that. When you do, you must still stay with him so that he doesn't get back up. If he does, you must do it all over again so that he doesn't get back into the play. It's the blocker's job to open holes for the runner, and he does it by applying these techniques: driving off the mark at the snap; hitting into the defender with his head and bringing his forearm and shoulder up into the man; keeping his legs under him and constantly moving; powering the man out of the way and opening the hole for the ball carrier. It used to be that the lineman had to keep his hands in, gripping his jersey on blocks, but now he isn't completely restricted this way. But be careful with those hands, because if you get them too close to the defensive man, the officials will call you for holding at times when you're not.

Blocking has been one of the subjects of debate since the beginning of football, as we learned in the first chapter, and even recently legislation has changed the game somewhat. Blockers no longer can hit a defensive man below the waist on a crackback block. I agree with this change, because the old crackback was causing an awful lot of knee injuries by guys coming out of nowhere to throw blindside blocks on linebackers and defensive ends. But I don't agree with those who are trying to take the head tackle and head block out of football. I dislike spearing a guy who is already down, but

This is an excellent example of drive blocking all across the offensive line. Our linemen have fired out off the snap, exploded into the defensive linemen, and continued driving their feet. Notice the posture of left tackle Art Shell (78), who is about to deliver his blow.

that comes under another category: hitting late, something that must be stopped. But tackling and blocking with the head has always been part of football. That's why we wear helmets and facemasks.

To summarize all of the techniques used at all positions, it all goes back to your basics. It's a personal thing, what's comfortable to you. And balance, plus performance, are the main factors. When you get tired, concentrate on your form, like runners in track. Late in a race, when they get tired, they work on style and technique rather than power, because that's waning. When you get tired and lose your style, you overexert yourself and waste energy. It is most important at this time to do things correctly. When you do things you normally wouldn't do, that's when you get into trouble. But when you concentrate on your techniques, you get the most production possible out of yourself.

# chapter six

BALANCED ATTACK—An offensive system that stresses running and passing almost equally.

CUTBACK—A running back heading in one direction turns back sharply in another direction.

DIVE PLAY—A quick-hitting play in which the quarterback hands the ball to a running back going straight into the line.

DOUBLE-THREAT—A player who can advance the ball by either running or throwing, like Pittsburgh quarterback Terry Bradshaw.

DRAW PLAY—A play that starts out looking like a pass and turns into a run when the quarterback hands off to a running back.

FINESSE ATTACK—One that relies on cunning and skill to beat a defense.

INFLUENCE PLAY—An offensive player draws a defender out of the area into which a play is to be run.

INTERFERENCE—Blocking to clear a lane for a runner.

OFF-TACKLE PLAY—A back takes the ball and runs through the tackle hole on either side of the line.

OPTION—The player carrying the ball has a choice of whether to pass or run the ball.

PLAY FAKE—The quarterback fakes a running play to hold the defense, then throws a pass.

POWER ATTACK—One that relies on brute strength.

PULLING LINEMAN—An offensive blocker who backs out of the line and leads a play around end.

QUICK TOSS—A lateral from the quarterback to a speedy running back for a fast-developing play around end.

SHIELD BLOCK—A blocker just gets in the way of an opponent to keep him out of a play.

SUCKER PLAY—A defensive player is fooled by a misdirection offensive fake and takes himself out of the play without being blocked.

SWEEP—A wide running play around end with several blockers out in front of the ball carrier.

TOTAL OFFENSE—Combined rushing and passing yards accumulated by an offense.

TRAP PLAY—A defensive player is drawn away from the direction of the play and is then blocked out of it when he sees his mistake.

TRIPLE OPTION—The offensive craze of the 1970s in college and high school, in which the quarterback has three choices of what to do with the ball.

# the running game

The late Vince Lombardi, great coach of the Green Bay Packers during their glory days in the 1960s, started out his chapter on the running game in his book on football by saying, "This is football." Of course, Mr. Lombardi was a lineman, an outstanding one, during his playing days. Being a quarterback on a passing team, I naturally am partial to the passing game, but I realize how much more effective the running game can make your passing.

The Raiders are, and always have been, known as a passing team, dating back to the days of the American Football League, when the game was almost all passing. But if you look at the statistics in recent years, you'll find that we have been right up there in rushing and total offense as well. We strive for a balanced attack, even though most of our biggest plays come on passes.

Even if you have a predominantly passing team, you can't go into any game and abandon running. I believe that you must run the ball to be able to throw it, and vice versa. In the games where we've had the most success in Oakland, we've had a balanced attack. No one has ever really shut down our passing game, so that means that we have to run the ball to achieve the balance we're looking for. We've had the most trouble in games where we couldn't run effectively.

The ground game is what controls a football game. You might get ahead with passing, but later in the game you must control the football if you're ahead. You can control the clock and keep the ball away from the other team if you can successfully run the ball and pass as well. When you can't run and are forced to rely on the pass, the defense knows what you're going to do. So does everyone in the stadium. You can't beat people consistently when they have a good idea what you're planning to do.

In that 1974 championship game we lost to Pittsburgh, we were able to run for just 29 yards, yet I was able to pass for more than 270. However, we were able to score just 10 points in the first three quarters, whereas the Steelers scored 21 in the final period to win 24-13. Had we been able to run the ball successfully, we would have scored more points and could have controlled the game. I might have passed for fewer yards because I wouldn't have had to throw 30 or so times, but maybe with the defense having to respect the run, I could have thrown for more yards in fewer attempts.

The running game opens up your offense. You can pass on first down if they have to respect the run, then run on second and third downs when they don't know exactly what to expect. It gives you the element of surprise. You can run or throw any time you want to, and the defense can't overplay one or the other.

Probably the biggest way the running game helps your passing is with play fakes. If you're running the ball well, you can fake a run and the defensive linemen and linebackers have to respect that fake. The linemen can't rush the quarterback recklessly right from the snap because they have to make sure it's not a run before they begin their pass rush. The linebackers must make sure before they drop back to help defend against the pass. This gives the quarterback more time to look for receivers downfield, and gives the receivers more room to maneuver between the linebackers and defensive backs.

Play fakes do you no good when you haven't been running the ball well, because the linemen can tee off and go straight for the quarterback. They don't have to respect your running fake. That puts the offense at a distinct disadvantage, because you can't rely just on passing against a good defense. We've had great success with play fakes in Oakland, but only when we've been able to establish the run.

There are many ways to use the running game. You can even use the pass to set up the run by employing play fakes early in the game so the other team is looking for the pass. Then you run on them. But usually your running game depends on the type of people you have on offense and the defense you're going against.

The Buffalo Bills have Jim Braxton, a big, strong fullback they use to hit inside on straight dives and off-tackle plays, things that suit him. They don't use him very often on a sweep because they have O. J. Simpson, the best runner in football, for that. They use their personnel in ways that are most effective.

It's the same with offensive linemen. If you have two mobile guards like Reggie McKenzie and Joe DeLamielleure to block for a fast guy like O. J., you're going to run a lot of sweeps. We have Gene Upshaw, and we use him for sweeps more than George Buehler, our other guard, because Gene is faster. But George is probably a little bit stronger and maybe better on straight-ahead blocking, so we use him on plays like that, though each of them can do both things.

Some teams have trouble defensing trap plays—their defensive linemen penetrate too quickly across the line—so you can make yards against them if you have good trap blockers. Or you can use quick-hitting plays against them. There are dozens of theories and ideas on the running game, but it depends on the kind of players you have.

We use Marv Hubbard, our big fullback, to run straight ahead behind guys like Art Shell, John Vella, Dave Dalby, and our other strong blockers. We use our quicker backs, Clarence Davis and Jess Phillips, on sweeps behind Upshaw. You have to fit the individ-

This is our version of the power sweep, with guards Gene Upshaw and George Buehler (64) leading for Jess Phillips against Cincinnati.

We like to run to the left behind All-Pro guard Gene Upshaw (63) and All-Pro tackle Art Shell (78) on the weak side (the tight end is on the right, or strong side in this case) even though people often know we will go that way. We'll send fullback Marv Hubbard (44) through the hole in front of halfback Clarence Davis (28), and that's formidable blocking power. The Raiders are known for their weak-side running.

ual characteristics of your players into your system.

People have said the Raiders are a left-handed team because I'm left-handed. That's not exactly true. We run often to our left because we have Upshaw and Shell, both of them All-Pro several times, over there. It makes sense. They didn't make the Pro Bowl by standing on their heads. We line up strong to the right and run to the weak-side behind those two guys, sometimes using Hubbard, a 240-pounder, as a lead blocker. That gives you some blocking punch. Then when the defense is looking for us to go that way, we've been able to go back to the right side, where Vella and Buehler are also outstanding blockers, and get good gains going that way. Those guys just aren't as experienced as Upshaw and Shell.

But we definitely do go more to the left. If you have people with those capabilities, you have to use them. It would be like not using Fred Biletnikoff and Cliff Branch, throwing to our tight end and backs most of the time. Or like Buffalo, which didn't use O. J. much when he first got there. When the Bills finally started doing it, look at the things he did. He could have done it all along. The good, solid running backs can gain yardage against anyone, even though many times the defense knows what's coming. They know O. J. is going to carry a lot, but even when defenses key on him, he gains yards. Defenses also know we like to run to the left, but even when they expect it, there are times that we break big plays.

I know that the running game isn't the most exciting part of football for fans. The only time it's exciting is when you break long runs for 40 or 50 yards. Yet that kind of run doesn't come very often because of the type of people teams have playing defense. But even though it's not always great to watch, the running game is a necessary and very important part of football. It can be dull, but the average fan must understand that it's the bread and butter of football.

All coaches will say it at one time or another: "We have to establish a game." I know it's a cliché, but it's true. I know at the beginning of the game that we're going to be in good shape if we're able to run the ball right away. It makes things happen on offense and we can control the tempo of the game. It sets up anything we want to do on offense. If you can't run, it puts your offense in a bind. All the advantage then lies with the defense.

Once you've established something by running the football, even if it's just in one area, it helps your offense. Say we've been making yards to the left side all day long on running plays, but it seems that we can't gain even a yard to the right. If I want to run a play-action pass, I'll call for the play fake to the left side: the people on that side of the defense have to respect it because we've been going that way for yards the entire game.

The running game determines your entire offense. If you can run, then you can pass; you can also play pass, and you can run draws and screen passes. Usually you find out early if you're going to be able to do all these things—use your entire offense—by the way your line is handling the other team. However, there are times when it takes a while, sometimes even until the second half, before you get things going. You can't get frustrated and abandon the running game if it isn't going. You have to give it a chance. Even if you don't gain many yards for the first five or six football plays you use, maybe for three or four series at the start of the game, you must keep trying. Sometimes you must make adjustments to get things moving.

The offensive line is the most important part of the running game, although a good back can make a line look good. Of course, a great back is going to get his yards regardless of his blockers; but without a good line, your running game is in trouble. In fact, your whole team is in trouble because that's where games are won and lost. The success of the Buffalo running game is based on the remarkable skills of O. J. Simpson, plus a fine offensive line. There are times when he makes them look good with outstanding individual runs, but there are many other times when they create openings for him. They would be a fine line blocking for any back.

As I've already pointed out, we have an outstanding line in Oakland, but in addition we have several good backs. We don't have one great back, but still we have a very good running game. We run the ball almost as well as anyone, and better than most teams. If you put a great back behind a mediocre line, he's going to get some yards on his own, but you won't have a successful running game. If you put O. J. with the worst line in football, he's going to get his yards because he's O. J. But he won't gain 2,000 or even 1,500 in a season.

Marv Hubbard certainly isn't a breakaway back, but he gained 1,100 yards for us in 1972; Pete Banaszak, Mark van Eeghen, and Hubbard gained over 1,500 and scored 20 touchdowns from the fullback spot in 1974. But it was the backs and the line working together that got those yards. I think there are several backs in the league who could gain 1,000 yards in our backfield. I don't think O. J. would gain 2,000, though, because with receivers like Fred Biletnikoff and Cliff Branch, we're going to throw a certain amount, too. You can't put them out to pasture. O. J. might gain, say, 1,400 with us, but then he could average perhaps seven yards per carry, because teams couldn't key on him as much with our passing game. O. J. carries the ball so much for Buffalo that 1,000 yards really isn't an accomplishment. Yet he averages five yards a carry, and that's something. That's the important thing when you look at rushing statistics.

There are different styles of running games. Some use mostly power, others are finesse-type attacks, and still others are a combination of both. The Raiders are basically a power running team. We don't do anything fancy. We have big and strong people on our front line and we attempt to run teams off the line. We run right at the defense, mostly with Upshaw and Shell, but we feel all of our linemen are like that.

The Pittsburgh Steelers aren't as big and strong on the offensive line, but they get things done with finesse. They can do that with Franco Harris at fullback. They toss the ball outside to Franco, or run him inside on trap plays. Their line is very good and very underrated, but they can do those things because of Franco. He runs out there and stops, then cuts back and goes for 25 or 30 yards. You just don't see many 235-pound guys who can do that. Franco is a great back, and he's hurt us a lot in his career.

The Los Angeles Rams are like that, too. They don't really try to knock you off the line. They use position-type blocks and run quick-toss and trap plays with Lawrence McCutcheon. But they do run some power stuff with Jim Bertelsen and Cullen Bryant, because

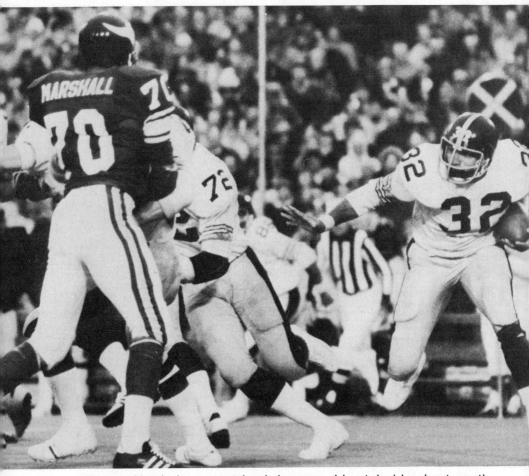

Franco Harris is a great back because his style blends strength and speed. Very few 235-pound backs can make a cutback like this and accelerate to full speed again. The Steeler linemen just try to stay in front of the defensive men, and Franco finds the holes. He's hurt us throughout his career.

they are more straight-ahead runners.

We've been talking quite a bit about Buffalo because they have the best back in the game. The Bills use a combination of finesse and power. Their offensive line is very flexible, and they have to be

O. J. Simpson is such a great back that he doesn't always need blocking to gain yardage. The blocker did not get to the defensive man in time on this play, but O. J. still got outside for yardage.

with Braxton running inside. They try to knock people out of there and let Braxton get into the secondary, running people over and carrying guys with him. But when they give the ball to O. J., all the linemen have to do is shield guys or get in the way for an instant, and O. J. is gone. Sometimes, when they fake to O. J. and give to Braxton, they don't even have to block for him because the whole defense is going after O. J. Their running game goes because of this balance, and Joe Ferguson's fine passing.

The running game is much more complicated in pro football than in high school and college. In high school and college, at least when I played, you just ran your offense and figured you were going to whip the defense. In the pros, defenses are much more sophisticated, plus you have great individuals who can control a game. This is especially true of some defensive linemen. You have to run plays to neutralize these guys, even if you don't gain an inch. Sometimes you accomplish much on plays like this.

When we play Pittsburgh, we like to run right at Mean Joe Greene or L. C. Greenwood, even if they stop the play cold, so they will respect the run and not rush the passer so much. These things accomplish something most of the time. We do it against Jerry Sherk of Cleveland, Lyle Alzado and Paul Smith of Denver, Elvin Bethea and Curley Culp of Houston, and anyone else who gives us any trouble. You can throw the ball better without having these guys in your face every time you go back to throw a pass. In high school and college football, you run your plays and you try to get your yards and first downs. You usually don't concern yourself with an individual defensive man.

The triple-option and veer-T offenses are very big right now in high school and college football. I ran the option in high school and in college, so I can see why these offenses are so popular. Texas, Oklahoma, and Alabama—many of the big-time college powers—are running these offenses with great results, so everyone is going to them. I can see several reasons why. For one thing, it's a very successful offense and also it's hard to defense. I've talked to several college coaches about it, and they tell me it really creates problems for a defense.

Most of the plays are run to the outside, so you have to string out your defense against it. Then if you overplay the offense to the strong side, they can run back to the weak side and kill you. Also, with most of the defense concentrated on the outside areas, if you have a big, fast fullback hitting into the middle, he can gain big yard-

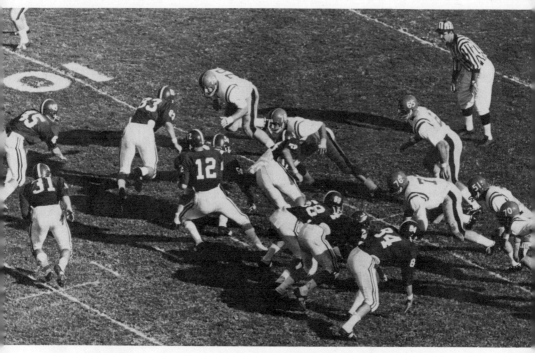

This is the way we ran the option play at Alabama. I could give the ball to the lead back (45), or run the ball myself around end, or run until the defense closed in and pitch out to the trailing back (31).

age because there aren't many defenders in there. You need a good running quarterback, a big fullback, and a couple of good backs. The offensive line doesn't have to be spectacular, just good and solid.

It's much easier to find a good running quarterback than a passing quarterback in high school and college. There just aren't that many hotshot passing quarterbacks coming out of high school, even though you come across them every now and then. It makes sense to have an offense predicated on the quarterback's running rather than his passing, although if he can do both, what it does is add another option to the triple option.

The passing game takes a lot more time to develop than the run-

91

ning game, especially in high school. You must have talented people at the skill positions, the backs and receivers. There is more timing involved. Plus, the most difficult thing to teach, at any age or level of football, is pass blocking. Even in high school, football comes down to your personnel. You do the things your players are best fit to do. In high school, your only quarterback might not be a very accomplished runner or passer, but rather is a team leader. You'd rather have him running than passing because more things can go wrong when you put the ball in the air.

These are some of the reasons why the triple option and running game are so big right now. But the running game always has been the biggest thing in high school football. When I played at Foley, I threw the ball perhaps ten times a game. I was a double-threat in those days. When we ran the straight option play, I would go down the line, fake to the fullback, and either keep the ball or pitch out to the trailing back. Now, in the triple option, all three backs are lined up behind the quarterback, and it gives you an extra option. It's a great offense, for high school and college, but I don't think you can run it in the pros because the defensive people are so big and quick. New England tried a bit of it a few years ago when Chuck Fairbanks came from Oklahoma to the Patriots. He even had Jack Mildren, his quarterback at Oklahoma, running it, but they abandoned it after a short trial.

I was a pretty good option quarterback, and I've always wondered what I could do with the triple option. I'd like to think I'd do all right if my knees were sound. Coach Bryant once said if we'd had the triple option when I was at Alabama, they would have had to put another digit on the scoreboard. Of course, as I said, I was a running quarterback back then. I've talked with him about the triple option, and he swears by it. Of course, Alabama always has a big, running quarterback, a big fullback, and all kinds of halfbacks, so it suits their personnel. You can't knock success. Alabama has been in the top five the last several years, and they're always in a bowl game. The success the triple option has had at the college level has led to its being an influence on the high schools, but that's OK because younger players learn early the importance of the running game. However, any team that runs it should have some sort of passing game, not only to complement the running game, but as a means of survival. The triple option can be the worst offense in the world if you get behind and are forced to come back. Without any passing game, you're in big trouble. That's why balance must be stressed in any attack.

In the present-day philosophy of the running game, the quarterback is not a blocker on running plays as he was in the early days of football. (George Blanda was a blocker at Kentucky in the 1940s.) So the offense ends up with nine men, excluding the quarterback and the ball carrier, to block against 11 defenders. In most systems, the other running back must be able to block when he doesn't have the ball, although that's not always true. With the Bills, Braxton always blocks for O. J., and at 240 pounds he can do an excellent job. I'm sure that O. J. tries to block for Braxton, but blocking isn't his bag. He's a 1,000-yard-plus back, and he's not really expected to block that much. I'm sure that O. J. rests on plays when he doesn't carry the ball, unless it's at a crucial point in the game or if his block is vitally important to the play. You have to expect that of a guy who's called on so much to carry the ball. You need him too much to take him out, yet he has to take a break once in a while.

Our system, like most others, is different. A halfback who can block is going to play a lot for us. Usually you think of the fullback as the lead blocker for the halfback, but as often as not it works the other way with the Raiders. Actually, both backs block for each other. But our offense is somewhat fullback-oriented, as O. J. pointed out when playing our system in the Pro Bowl, and a super blocker such as Clarence Davis is so valuable. C. D. weighs 195 pounds, but he blocks successfully against guys 250 or more. We played Minnesota a few years ago, and he stood Carl Eller straight up on one play I remember. Of course, if we could somehow get O. J., I'm sure we could make some adjustments. It would be foolish not to.

The running game is a team type of thing. But there are some instances when your halfback is not involved in the blocking, yet he influences a defensive man to go away from the play. Look at the six diagrams in this chapter and you'll notice that on the examples of power offense, the back not carrying the ball is a blocker. By con-

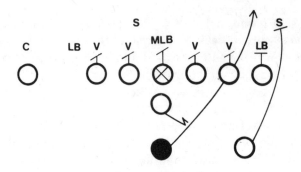

Diagram 15
Fullback off-tackle (46)

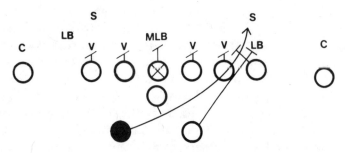

Diagram 16
Halfback off-tackle (36)

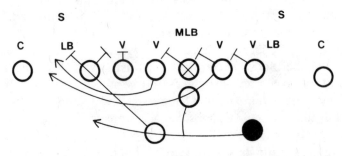

Diagram 17
Power sweep left (27)

POWER RUNNING GAME

trast, on the examples of finesse offense, the other back does not block but instead is employed somewhat as a decoy to lure a linebacker and any other defensive men away from the spot where the play actually is headed. That doesn't mean that the other back in a finesse offense never blocks. At Pittsburgh, which uses finesse-type plays, Rocky Bleier blocks well and often for Franco Harris.

However, in the power offense, everyone generally has a defensive man to block and each block is important. Look at diagram 15 and notice that the halfback blocks on the safety. That's maybe the biggest block on that play because the fullback runs right in behind it. When the fullback clears the line of scrimmage, the first guy waiting would be the safety. If the halfback misses him, the play most likely won't work. In diagram 16, the halfback blocks on the linebacker to spring the fullback. In diagram 17, a sweep play, the fullback helps seal off the inside pursuit of the defense. (We'll break down these plays in complete detail a little later.)

Now for the finesse offense: in diagram 18, notice how the halfback fakes a quick toss to the right in order to fool the defense. In diagram 19, the draw play, the halfback runs a deep pass pattern up the sideline to take the linebacker away from the course of the fullback. On the trap play, diagram 20, the fullback fakes the quick toss to influence the right side of the defense, and the halfback carries the ball through the area those defensive men vacated to chase the fullback. In some offenses, one back or the other may be designated as the blocking back, but in all offenses, it's vitally important that the back without the ball assist in the correct functioning of every play.

Now that you have a good background on the working parts of a running play, and have the basics of offense from the simple system we mapped out in Chapter Three, let's run through some more plays. As already explained, diagrams 15-17 are plays from a power offense, while diagrams 18-20 are finesse plays. The differences should be easily recognizable.

The first play (diagram 15) is a fullback off-tackle play, or in the jargon of the basic offense you already learned, a 46. The four back will carry the ball through the six hole. But first, everyone on offense must do his job. We'll run all these plays against a basic 4-3

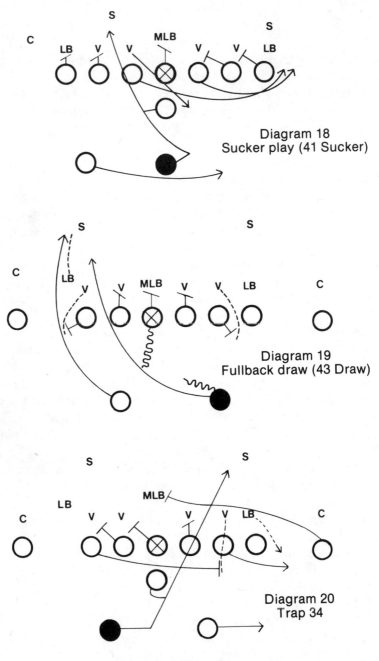

Diagram 18
Sucker play (41 Sucker)

Diagram 19
Fullback draw (43 Draw)

Diagram 20
Trap 34

FINESSE RUNNING GAME

pro defense, with four defensive linemen, three linebackers, and four defensive backs. The fullback off-tackle is a relatively basic power play. The offensive linemen all block the defensive men opposite them, and the center fires out to get the middle linebacker. The right tackle may try to take his man inside and the tight end may try to move his man out, but basically they just try to knock them back off the line. The halfback leads through and blocks the safety whichever way he can, and the fullback cuts inside or outside, depending on where the open area develops.

Diagram 16 is our old 36 play that we ran in Chapter Three, with the halfback carrying behind the fullback to the tackle hole on the right. The blocking is the same as on the 46 play, except that the tight end and the right tackle put a double-team block on the defensive end, moving him to the inside. The fullback comes through and kicks out the linebacker, the halfback cutting upfield off that block.

Your basic power sweep is shown in diagram 17. Almost everybody runs this play, even the finesse teams. In your offense from Chapter Three, it would be called a 27, with the halfback carrying around left end. The center snaps the ball and tries to cut off the tackle to his left—a difficult block, but usually all he has to do is slow the man down. The two guards pull out of the line to lead interference around left end, the left guard taking the first man outside and the right guard the first man inside. The right tackle blocks on the defensive tackle, but the rest of the defensive men on that side are left alone. The left tackle blocks the defensive end in front of him and the tight end takes the linebacker. The fullback comes in right behind the tight end and blocks anyone coming across from the middle, attempting to screen anyone else coming that way out of the play. The quarterback makes a reverse pivot and a 180-degree turn, as he does on all three of these power plays, and gives to the halfback, who turns the corner and looks for the biggest hole in the defense and a possibility of breaking outside.

Moving on to the finesse offense, take a look at diagram 18, the sucker play. In simple terms, you can call this a 41, but that's where the simplicity ends. This play is supposed to look like a quick pitch and a sweep to the right. Both guards pull to the right, causing the defensive tackles, especially the one on the offense's left side, to

Here's how the draw play works (above and facing page). The quarterback drops as if to pass, but notice I don't have the ball gripped in my left, or throwing, hand. That's because I'm going to hand off to Clarence Davis, who has delayed a bit, on the draw.

read it as a sweep and flow with the guards. The tackle and tight end on the left block the defensive end and the linebacker to the outside. The center again fires out to cut off the middle linebacker. The quarterback fakes the toss to the halfback going right and turns to hand off to the fullback, who had also started right but now cuts back to the spot the defensive tackle left open. The defensive tackle was "suckered" into believing the play was to be a sweep and we never blocked him at all. We finessed him.

The fullback draw, diagram 19, is meant to look like a pass play, so the offensive linemen set up in pass blocking initially and take each defensive man the way he wants to go. The quarterback drops back to pass while the fullback takes two steps and stops to the right of the quarterback. At the last instant, the quarterback turns and hands to the fullback. The halfback has run a deep pass pattern to take out the left linebacker and the center has fired out on the middle linebacker. The play is designed to go over the left guard hole, a 43, but the fullback just searches for the most promising opening and gets there as quickly as possible. This play often goes for big yardage, since the defense reads pass at the outset. The linemen are rushing the quarterback; the backs are dropping back to cover the receivers and have their backs turned to the play. If the fullback clears the line of scrimmage, he's usually got lots of room. Again, we fooled the defense, we didn't overpower them.

The trap play is perhaps the most often-used finesse play. Run off the right side by the halfback as in diagram 20, it's a 34. As with the sucker play, it's supposed to influence the defense into believing it's a toss play, or something wide to the right. But the defensive end on that side is the key man this time. The offensive tackle pulls as if to lead blocking for the fullback around right end. That leaves a hole open for the offensive end to penetrate into the backfield, just what we want him to do. The linebacker on that side also flows out to take care of the toss, clearing out that area. Our right guard takes care of the defensive tackle, while the center and left guard cut off the defensive linemen on the other side. The tight end, lined up on the right, goes out and cuts off the middle linebacker. After faking the toss to the fullback, the quarterback turns and gives the ball to the halfback cutting inside. Even if the defensive tackle realizes his mistake, it's too late, because when he turns to come back, our left tackle has come all the way down the line to block him out of the play. He's trapped.

As you have seen, there are many phases to the running game. But again, it comes down to personnel. If you have quick guys on the offensive line and a shifty back, you should use a finesse attack, though occasionally you can use a power play. If you have big, strong linemen, you're best to use a power game. But whatever you do, you must be effective with your basic running plays to make the rest of your offense operative. The running game affects all phases of offense, what you can and can't do. In pro football, almost every team can throw the football to a certain extent, but not every team can run the football. The teams that can are the successful ones.

Even if you have a superior passing attack, consistency on offense is achieved only when you have a solid ground game to go with it. Quarterbacks may favor the passing game, but a smart one will never de-emphasize his running attack. The two are like sugar and spice. We'll go right on to the spice now.

# chapter seven

BLITZ—A linebacker rushes the quarterback.

BREAK—A receiver's cut on a passing play.

BURNER—A pass receiver with exceptional speed.

BURST—A sudden explosion of speed by a receiver downfield to reach a pass.

CLEAR OUT—A receiver runs through a zone and takes the defender there with him, opening the area for another receiver.

COVERAGE—Pass defense used by the defensive secondary.

DECOY—A receiver who is not meant to receive the pass but instead draws defenders away from other receivers.

DROP AREAS—Zones the linebackers slide back into in defensive pass coverage.

DROP BACK—The quarterback goes straight back to pass.

FLAT—The short, outside passing area.

ISOLATION—A receiver is left one-on-one with a defensive man, often a running back-linebacker mismatch.

MOVE—The fake a receiver puts on a defensive back in order to get open for a pass.

NEUTRAL ZONE—The blocking area ranging five yards on each side of the line of scrimmage.

PASS BLOCKING—The protection the line and backs give the quarterback on passing downs.

PASS ROUTE—The exact path a receiver takes while running downfield on a pass play.

PASS RUSH—The line charge of the defense to get at the quarterback.

POCKET—The semicircle of protection a quarterback is given by his line, also called the passing cup.

PRIMARY RECEIVER—The man designated as the most likely to receive the pass on a certain play.

READING—Observing and understanding the opponent's tactics while the play is developing.

SCREEN PASS—A pass behind the line of scrimmage in which the receiver has a wall of blockers in front of him.

SECONDARY RECEIVER—A player who runs his pattern on a pass play but is not expected to get the ball unless the quarterback cannot get it to the primary receiver.

STUNTS—Adjustments in the pass rush by the defense in an attempt to fool the offensive line or catch it off balance.

# the passing game

As the quarterback, my job, basically, is to run the show on offense. But when you get right down to it, this is my baby—the passing game. They pay running backs for carrying the ball, linemen for blocking, and receivers for catching the ball. I make my living throwing the football and understanding how the entire passing game works. This is the part of football I enjoy most.

It hasn't always been that way, because in high school and college, we were basically running teams. I threw the ball five, six, eight times a game in high school, and 12 to 15—maybe 18 on the outside—at Alabama. I've always done what the coaches wanted me to do, and that's important for a quarterback, especially in high school and college. You're not qualified to tell your coach, "I want to run, or I want to throw more," at that stage.

103

In pro ball, it is somewhat different. Once a guy has been around a while and played the game, he knows enough about the game to suggest different things. And a coach isn't going to tell Johnny Unitas or Fran Tarkenton what to do, especially when it comes to the passing game, because the quarterback is the one who experiences and knows what goes on out on the field.

Again going back to Vince Lombardi's book, he said that the running game is dependent on all 11 men doing the job, while a successful passing play sometimes depends on only three or four guys. I agree and disagree. Say, for example, that on a sweep to the right, the left tackle misses a block. The defensive lineman isn't going to get across the field quick enough to stop that play. But if the tackle misses his man on a passing play, the ball may never be thrown because the quarterback might get sacked.

But on another passing play, one receiver might fall down at the line of scrimmage, yet the pass is completed. I understand what Lombardi was saying, but I think it's equally important on the run and the pass. You strive for 11 guys to do their job on every play. And you definitely can't rely on just five or six.

Although the running game is more complicated than the average fan might think, as we saw in the last chapter, it's basically one guy carrying the ball and the others blocking. The passing game isn't quite that simple. The quarterback takes the snap and drops back, but when he looks downfield the only thing he sees is a myriad of colors. There are guys running every which way, and it's his job to figure out this puzzle.

He might use decoy receivers to clear defenders out of a certain area. If the primary receiver is covered, he'll have to pick out a secondary receiver who is open. In addition to the tight end and wide receivers, he might send his backs on pass routes. All of these pass patterns must complement each other, because if two receivers are in the same area, it means two or more defenders will also be there. You can't have two guys running 20-yard outs. And while all of this is going on, the quarterback must get enough pass protection from the offensive line to sit back there and pick out a receiver. Without any time, the play most likely won't work.

Passing plays are more complicated than running plays because

I've just let go of the ball, but already I'm headed upfield because I know Fred Biletnikoff is going to catch it for a first down. You get this kind of feeling with a receiver only after working with him for several years.

several players have more than one assignment. A back may stay in at first to watch for blitzes by the linebackers or to pick up any pass rusher who may get past a blocker, but then the back may release on a pass route. The tight end also throws a block before he goes out on a pass pattern. The wide receiver is just the opposite. First he runs his pattern—in which he may be used to clear out an area—but when the pass is completed to another receiver, he becomes a down-field blocker. The offensive linemen are pass blocking in the neutral zone and can't release downfield until the ball is thrown. If they leave too soon, there is a penalty. But when the pass is completed in the short or intermediate zone, they also may become downfield blockers.

We've already said that the offensive line is the key to the run-

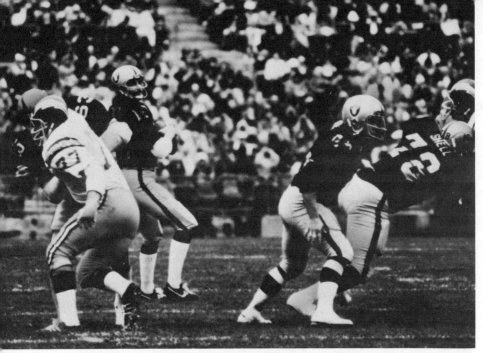

If the offensive line can give the quarterback protection like this for three to four seconds, the receivers are going to have time to get open and the quarterback will have time to pick them out and get the ball there. This is the biggest strength of our team—pass blocking.

ning game, but with the passing game, it's even more important. As the great running back will get his yards even without blocking, the great passing quarterback will get a lot of yards on his own talent. But when he doesn't get the ball off, it's a 10-yard loss, and you just can't overcome long-yardage situations all the time. Again, this is why people in football say that games are decided in the line. Whichever line controls the game will usually win.

Our line in Oakland, which is rated one of the top lines in football, works hard for balance, but because of the nature of our team, they're probably better at pass blocking. Though they are also very good at blocking for the run, they realize that I'm not as mobile as I used to be so they protect me well. Also, this is the way we win games, by throwing the football. We're a high-percentage passing team and score a lot of touchdowns that way. We can jump out to an early lead or come from behind to win with our passing game. So our guys know they must pass protect, and as I said earlier, this is probably the toughest thing to teach in football.

The offensive line sets up what is called "the pocket" to protect

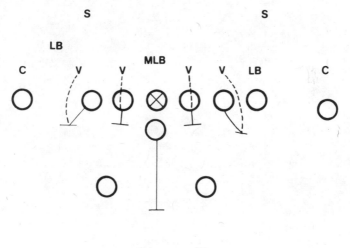

Diagram 21
The pocket

its quarterback (see diagram 21). It's important that the quarterback stay in the pocket as long as possible. It's the ideal place from which to throw the ball. If the quarterback remains in the pocket, the offensive linemen know where he is at all times and can block their men accordingly. As you see in the diagram, the defensive ends generally rush to the outside. This isn't always true, but two pass rushers usually take these rushing lanes. The offensive tackle just rides the rusher to the outside, carrying him past the quarterback. The guards charge straight ahead. They can't allow any penetration in the middle because the quarterback must be able to step up into the pocket if the ends get close. The center, unless he has a lineman rushing directly over him, usually helps out wherever needed and picks up blitzes and stunts.

As you can see by the diagram, the line forms a semicircle of protection for the quarterback. As long as they sustain their blocks, he's safe in there. If the quarterback strays to the right or left, he runs into the defensive charge. Of course, when a defensive man breaks in, the quarterback must scramble. He has no choice. The

This is what happens when the pocket breaks down, as our defensive guys show Cleveland's Mike Phipps, who is being buried by Horace Jones, Phil Villapiano, Otis Sistrunk, and Gerald Irons.

quarterback can feel during the game if he's getting good protection or not. You can feel a defensive lineman getting close. But you can't stop and look directly at the rush because you must concentrate on what is going on downfield. When a defensive end is getting close, you simply step up into the pocket. But when the pocket breaks down in the middle, the quarterback must get out.

We've established that you *control* a game with your running attack; but you *win* games—most of the time—by throwing the football. Games are won with big plays, and most of them are passes, since you don't have that many 50- and 60-yard runs. Even though I said that the teams who run in pro football are the teams who win, in most cases, pro football is a passing game. Those who run effectively can win games with big passing plays. Pittsburgh is a good example. Every time they've beaten us, the Steelers have run first and then scored big touchdowns with the pass. They send Franco Harris into the line 25 or 30 times and then Terry Bradshaw will throw a TD to Lynn Swann or John Stallworth.

Miami was like that, too. That's how the Dolphins went undefeated in 1972. It was their formula for winning two consecutive

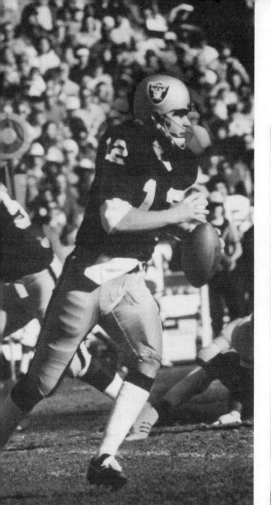

The quarterback must know when to get out of the pocket if he feels it is going to break down. You won't often see me scrambling like this, but when I am forced out I still look for the pass because a broken play gives the receiver more of a chance to get open. The defender doesn't know whether to come up for the run or stay with the receiver—and often he's caught in between.

Super Bowls. They'd run Larry Csonka into the line again and again until you'd get them in a third-and-four situation, when they still would run Csonka for the first down—but somewhere along the way, Bob Griese would hit Paul Warfield for a touchdown. You keep the ball moving with the running game; you get your big plays throwing.

Those great Green Bay teams were another example. Bart Starr would run Jim Taylor and Paul Hornung all day, then throw in a little play fake and hit Max McGee for a TD. They won two Super Bowls that way, and Starr, like Griese, sometimes wouldn't throw more than 10-12-15 times, but he might have three or four TD passes. I like that type of system. If we have to throw 30 times in a game, we're in trouble. It's difficult to depend on passing alone.

More big games are won by passing than by running. When you have two evenly matched teams, that's usually where the game is decided. I remember a game when I was a junior in college, against Louisiana Tech. We ran the ball all day and I threw only five passes. Only two of them were complete, but they were good for 111 yards and two TDs. We won 34-0 and you can't really say we beat them passing. But we put the game out of reach with those passes after we'd run the ball successfully.

Being able to throw the football is something that's a God-given talent, but also it can be worked on and improved. At 16 or 17 years old, I didn't understand this, so I may not have done as much work on it as I should have. We were a running team, so I'd go out onto the field and run-and-cut, dodge around guys, and pitch out to someone else. I wish now that I had thrown more, and not just in games. If you establish that you can throw the ball pretty well, you should play catch as much as possible. This strengthens your arm and improves your accuracy. Throw it long and short, in and out, everywhere. Get to where you feel comfortable throwing the ball. Don't worry about throwing a perfect spiral every time, just get the ball there. Once you've thrown the ball for a long period of time, you should throw good passes naturally almost every time. But this just comes from hard work.

If you can throw a 15-yard bullet, work to be able to throw one 25 yards. Get together with your receivers during the summer, or any time outside of regular practice, in gym class or whatever, and have them run their patterns. This way you'll learn what type of pass you'll need to throw on each given pattern and you will learn your receivers' every move. But throw the ball, to anyone, whenever you can. I never put up a swinging tire and tried to throw through it, but that's good, too, if you want to throw by yourself.

Even though I didn't throw the ball as much on my own as I maybe should have when I was a kid, I was always able to do well passing the ball because I guess I just had a natural ability to throw a ball. I'm not bragging, but I was also a pitcher in baseball and a shooter in basketball, so every sport that I played I was throwing the ball one way or another. I was a control pitcher and a high-percentage shooter, so I'm sure these things helped me become an accurate passer. It all goes back to hand-and-eye coordination. That sort of thing just came easy to me.

Not much has remained constant about the passing game from high school to college and into pro football. It's been completely different for me, even though some of the terminology is the same. There have always been ins, outs, curls, posts, slants, and comebacks, but the idea behind them isn't the same from high school to college or from college to the pros. The patterns get longer as you go along, because the players are stronger and faster. What is a curl one place might be a hook somewhere else. The philosophies are as different as night and day. In my case, the offense was still pretty simple, but definitely very effective, in college. Football has come a long way in the past 15 years.

I'm sure that the high school offenses that you'll be exposed to are more complicated than some of the things that we did in 1960. I've seen some high school games lately—the players did many things we didn't even know about. The coaches are more knowledgeable and there are more of them. We had three varsity coaches. Some teams now have nearly 10. Coaches can go to clinics to hear Bear Bryant of Alabama, Darrell Royal of Texas, or Mike White of California speak about a certain phase of the game. All of this is passed on to the players.

Some coaches give their quarterbacks the entire offense in the 10th grade and have them learn it as they go along, as they play it.

Other coaches give them more offense as they grow and mature mentally as well as physically. Either way can be good. But, I can tell you from experience, the best way to learn something is to do it yourself.

If you're a quarterback and your team doesn't throw much in high school, don't get frustrated, because I really wasn't a passer until my senior year in college. It was quite by accident, because, as I've said, we were a running team and I was a running quarterback. But then I hurt my knee in spring practice before my senior year, and it was then that I really became a passer. I knew that I couldn't depend on my running any more, so we became more of a passing team. I rushed for 397 yards as a junior and only 193 the next season. That made me a better passer. I passed 114 times as a junior for 956 yards, but the next season I passed 178 times for 1,214 yards. It was better for the team that we throw and it really helped me in the long run.

Another thing that has aided me throughout my career is that I've been blessed with outstanding receivers. That's something that's essential for great success with the passing game. I had good receivers in high school, but I didn't need them as much then because we didn't depend on our passing. It all began at Alabama, where we had Ray Perkins and Dennis Homan as our wide receivers when I was a junior. Perkins graduated that year and went on to play several seasons with the Baltimore Colts, where he became one of Johnny Unitas' favorite receivers. Homan was All-Southeastern Conference twice, All-American, and the No. 1 draft choice of the Dallas Cowboys. He played with Dallas, then with the Kansas City Chiefs, and caught over 40 passes with the Birmingham Americans of the World Football League before retiring We had a little guy named Richard Brewer who was an excellent college receiver—but too small for the pros—who also helped me.

But I believe that the group of receivers we have with the Raiders may be the best group ever assembled. We have Fred Biletnikoff, Cliff Branch, Mike Siani, and Morris Bradshaw as wide receivers—and tight ends Dave Casper and Ted Kwalick. All could start for just about any team in football.

A great passing quarterback will do all right even with mediocre

This is the greatest catch I've ever seen, made by Fred Biletnikoff in the 1974 playoffs against Miami. It's not obvious at first, but Tim Foley is holding onto Fred's right arm (you can see Fred's right hand just to the right of Foley's belt). But Freddie is just concentrating on the ball. He knows where he is at all times, and has a knack for keeping both feet inbounds on sideline passes.

receivers, but there are certain receivers who can make a quarterback look good on a bad throw. Biletnikoff is like this. He has great hands and he also has concentration, perhaps the most important ingredient a good receiver has. I've thrown passes that would ordinarily have been intercepted, incomplete, or out of bounds, but because of his exceptional ability, Fred has turned them into completions. If you give him an even break, he's going to catch the ball.

Freddie made a catch in the 1974 playoff game against Miami that was the greatest I've ever seen. He was in the corner of the end zone with cornerback Tim Foley hanging all over him. In fact, Foley had a hold on Fred's right arm and they were falling out of bounds, but Freddie still caught the ball with his free hand. It was the greatest catch I've ever seen, but I wasn't surprised that he made it. He never surprises me anymore. If I throw a ball to him and he's coming off his break, I know it's complete. The ball is in the air, but I start running upfield thinking about the next play. I know it's going to be first down. I don't feel that way about any other receiver, even though Cliff is getting there. It's something that's acquired by working with a guy over a period of years. I've been working with Fred, Cliff and Mike since I became a starter.

That's why knowing your receivers is so important. I've been to the Pro Bowl twice, with all the best receivers in the American Football Conference on my team, yet I had trouble both times because I didn't always know what they were going to do. Every receiver does things a little bit differently. A quarterback must study his receivers so he knows the characteristics of each. Then, in a game situation, he can read them correctly. We try to teach our receivers to do things the same way, but everybody runs differently, or has a different head and shoulder movement. Everyone has a distinctive style, like a fingerprint. The quarterback has to learn that if a guy does a certain thing, it means he's going to go in, or out, because defensive coverage can change a pattern while it's in motion and it's up to the quarterback to read it. The receivers do have the same footwork and get to the same area on a given pattern, but the getting there varies. After playing several years with my receivers, I know them pretty well because I've studied them. They know me, too, but we learn new things about each other all the time.

Receivers fall into two basic categories. The first one is the type with moves and intelligence, a finesse receiver. Fred Biletnikoff is the best of these in football. He runs a 4.7 40-yard dash, not the fastest, so he knows he must rely on his smarts and quickness. He can turn a defensive back inside-out with his moves. Freddie also reads defense expertly and knows where to be and when to get there. He also runs his patterns several different ways, so if a defender begins to catch on to a certain move, he can run the same pattern but do it in a different way. But Fred also has enough speed to get deep if the defense plays him too tight.

114

Cliff Branch is known as a burner because of his great speed, but coming to the Raiders and learning from Fred Biletnikoff has helped him immensely to develop as an exceptional all-around receiver. Here he's catching a pass in the middle of the fine Cincinnati secondary.

The other type is the burner, and you can't find much better than Cliff Branch. He's in that category with guys like Paul Warfield, Isaac Curtis, and Mel Gray. The best thing that happened to Cliff was coming to the team that has Biletnikoff. You can't teach anyone the 9.2 speed that Cliff has, but he's learned from Fred how to use moves to get open short as well. And Cliff is going to get better, because he'll get smarter the more experience he gets.

Having this type of diversity in our receivers makes it easy for me. People know that if we're going to go long, we probably will use Cliff. They have to play off him, so he gets open short. Freddie gets

Cincinnati has Ken Anderson, a very accurate and prolific passer, so the Bengals are going to throw the ball a lot. Anderson is adept at throwing long, intermediate, and short passes. Here he is on a flare to a back, which helps make up for a mediocre running game.

all kinds of coverage, but still catches 40 or 50 balls every year. They play up close on him and he still gets open. When we feel they're too close, we sneak him deep for big gainers. He's caught a lot of touchdowns that way.

The Raiders have a reputation as a passing team. We're right up there every year in the passing stats, and that goes way back to 1963 when Al Davis first came to Oakland. Even though John Madden runs the team, we still use the passing attack that Davis developed. A team would be stupid not to pass with quarterbacks like Tom Flores, Cotton Davidson, Daryle Lamonica, George Blanda and myself throwing to receivers like Art Powell, Clem Daniels, Biletnikoff, Hewritt Dixon, Warren Wells, Raymond Chester, Branch, and Siani.

As with the running game, every team has its own style of passing. But, again, it's based on personnel. Cincinnati isn't going to beat anyone running the ball, so they have Ken Anderson back there throwing all the time and gaining 3,000 yards. Yet, when Paul Brown (who retired as the Bengals' coach after the 1975 season) was in Cleveland, the Browns were a predominantly running team with the great Jimmy Brown carrying the ball. Oakland has had passers and receivers, so the Raiders have thrown the ball. I wasn't as aware of the Raiders' passing history as I was of the fact that they were a winning team when they drafted me, but I could see after I'd been with them a short while that I was going to enjoy playing within their system.

But even within that system, I do things a bit differently from the way Daryle Lamonica did. I'm most effective with the intermediate pass, at 15-18-20 yards. That's my bread-and-butter pass, but we mix in screens and some short stuff with bombs to Cliff. Daryle had a great arm and he could throw those crossfield outs, short corners, and all the deep passes extremely well. Lamonica was a picture passer. He and Warren Wells complemented each other perfectly. Warren caught 42 touchdown passes in just over three years, and I don't believe anyone in the history of football has ever done that. He was super-fast, could break off a move and go to the post faster than anyone I've ever seen. And he had an incredible burst to the ball way downfield. Wells just left defensive backs behind, even fast guys. Daryle would just let the ball go and Warren would get it. I remember a play they ran in the final minutes of a game against San Diego. We were behind and down around our own 20-yard line when Wells ran a post pattern. Daryle slipped and fell when he set up to pass, but Wells kept on going while the defender slowed up a bit. Daryle got up and threw the ball almost 80 yards in the air and Wells caught it for the game-winning TD. I believe that if Warren hadn't got into those personal problems that shortened his career, he would have been one of the very best ever to play football. He had that something special.

There are finesse passing attacks and power passing attacks, just

Fran Tarkenton and the Minnesota Vikings run a finesse-type passing game, often throwing short to their running backs to get them into the open field. This one is going to Ed Marinaro, but they also use Chuck Foreman, who can be devastating on this kind of play.

as with the running game. The Minnesota Vikings run a finesse attack with Fran Tarkenton. The Vikings throw short stuff to their backs, Chuck Foreman and Ed Marinaro, who combined to make about 90 receptions in 1975. They screen a great deal and run draw plays off the pass and play-action passes. They hit Stu Voight, their tight end, in the middle with short stuff, and used John Gilliam (now with Atlanta), one of the fine receivers in the game, for intermediate and occasionally long stuff. Coach Bud Grant and his people realize that Tarkenton is getting older and can't throw as far as he used to, but is still as accurate as ever. They've adapted that into their style of play.

Kansas City used a finesse-type game with Len Dawson at quarterback, using all those formations, shifts, and play fakes, but it was somewhat of a power attack when the ball went to Otis Taylor, who is large for a wide receiver at 6-4 and at least 215 pounds. Washington has a finesse attack with Billy Kilmer, who doesn't

Joe Namath is strictly a drop-back passer. He stands in the pocket and throws medium and long-range passes to Richard Caster and his other fine receivers, though Joe occasionally will drop the ball off to his backs to keep the defense honest.

throw as well as most quarterbacks in the league but who gets more out of his game than almost anybody. Kilmer is an extremely accurate short passer; they have him throw that quick slant to Charley Taylor, who used to be a running back and can take the punishment. Taylor will get up and run another one in there. Then, when the defense is looking for this, Kilmer will slip one of his receivers deep and get him wide open for a big gain.

The San Francisco 49ers are a finesse passing team, and when they had John Brodie at quarterback, they ran the screen pass better than anyone. Brodie would play pass and then screen, or even fake a screen on one side and run one on the other in the same play. They were so good at it that they twice scored touchdowns against us with it. John David Crow and Doug Cunningham, not your fastest backs by any means, went 60 or 70 yards to score.

We're a power passing team, just letting our big offensive line pass protect and not running play fakes unless we have to. We come right at you. The New York Jets have been like that for many years. Joe Namath goes straight back, sets up, and has receivers like Richard Caster, Jerome Barkum, and Eddie Bell. Namath has a strong arm, so he's going to throw deep corners, outs, posts, and bend-ups deep downfield. That's his style and therefore it's the Jets' style. Cincinnati is a combination of both styles since the Bengals throw the ball so much. They have Isaac Curtis and a number of good receivers, and they utilize all of them in every different way. Anderson is effective with all types of passes.

Though all teams have certain aspects of the passing game that every other team has, each club has its own system to make the most of the material it has to work with. Everyone has short, intermediate, and long passing routes, but each team has its own idea of how to use each part of its game. For instance, the Redskins like to send Charley Taylor, Jerry Smith, and their other receivers into the middle because they are big, strong guys. We hardly ever send Biletnikoff and Branch in there because these guys aren't that big and can't absorb that punishment consistently. We send our tight ends in there, because at 225 pounds and up, they're made for that.

We'll diagram some passing plays so you can get the idea of how the passing game works. The first three plays are typical short passing plays. In diagram 22, we send the halfback 10 yards into the left flat, the fullback curls over the middle at about six yards, and the flanker on the left side runs a post pattern 15 yards downfield to clear out that side for the halfback. The tight end runs an out at four yards and the right side wide receiver does a turn-in pattern at 15 yards. Very simple and basic.

Diagram No. 23 is the same type of idea, only nobody is clearing out an area. All we're doing is getting a back isolated on a linebacker, and with that kind of matchup, the back should be able to get free. That's the kind of mismatch the quarterback always looks for. The other receivers just take their defenders with them, out of the area of the pass. These are just two variations of the short game, using backs. But you can also use your wide receivers and tight end in the short passing game.

In diagram 24, we're throwing quick outs to the wide receivers. With a player like Cliff Branch, if the defender comes up too quick-

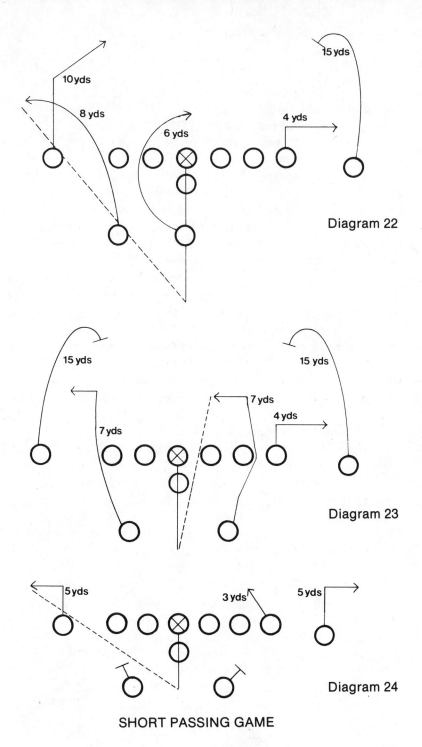

10 yds

8 yds

6 yds

4 yds

15 yds

Diagram 22

15 yds

7 yds

7 yds

7 yds

4 yds

15 yds

Diagram 23

5 yds

3 yds

5 yds

Diagram 24

SHORT PASSING GAME

121

ly and over-runs the play, it might turn into a big play. But this also can be a dangerous play, especially if the cornerback is playing up tight. He might intercept and it could turn out to be a touchdown for the defensive team.

Even though these plays are diagrammed here in the Raiders' system and formations, they can be adapted to any offense, even simpler ones used in high school and college. They don't necessarily have to be run from these formations, either. There are a million things you can do with the passing game. If you wanted to, you could run them from a full-house backfield.

In our short passing game, we throw the ball 10 yards and under. Next, when we go to the intermediate passing game, the ball is thrown somewhere between 12 and 18 yards. Long passes are balls that are thrown more than 20 yards. But these figures are very flexible. If a back comes out of the backfield and the quarterback is chased and can't get the ball off as soon as he wants, it can turn out to be a long gainer. That's what happened on that Lamonica-to-Wells bomb. On the other hand, a receiver is taught to work back toward the quarterback in other situations, and a long pass may turn into an intermediate play.

In diagram 25, we're throwing the ball 15 yards downfield to the tight end, who is running a turn-in. To get the tight end open in there, we run the wide receiver on the left side into the middle on a post pattern to occupy the safeties. Because the play is diagrammed this way, however, doesn't mean the tight end will always be the receiver. There are primary and secondary receivers on each play. What the defense does, and who gets open the quickest, determines whom you throw to. If the safety comes up and covers the tight end, you might throw to that wide receiver on a post pattern, making it a long pass of maybe 35 yards instead of an intermediate-type pass.

Diagram 26 is a common out route, which everybody runs. Both wide receivers go 15 yards downfield and break to the outside. If they are covered, this should leave the tight end open and he's running a hook pattern in there. The backs are running hooks at about six or eight yards. It puts a lot of pressure on the defense to cover all of these receivers well.

122

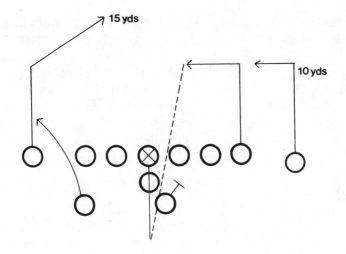

Diagram 25

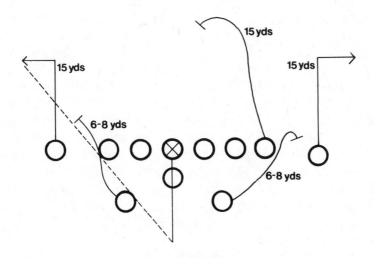

Diagram 26

INTERMEDIATE PASSING GAME

The final two diagrams are of the long passing game. In diagram 27, both the tight end and right-side wide receiver are breaking off post moves at about 20 yards. The ball is thrown out in front of them on this play at anywhere from 30 to 45 yards, occasionally even farther. It depends on how far the quarterback can throw the ball and how fast the receiver is. The left-side receiver is running a short corner, while the back is running about five yards into the flat in case the other receivers don't get open. Our backs are taught just to get into the flat area, turn to face the quarterback, and stop until the ball is delivered.

Diagram 28 is just a bend-up to the right-side wide receiver, a play we use often with Cliff Branch for big gains because of his blazing speed. This play is designed to go for a touchdown. The receiver breaks out to the sideline at 15 yards and then turns up the field at full speed. This play is a big part of our offense because our wide receivers run their comeback routes off this pattern. The receiver runs full-speed up the field, making the defender believe he is going deep. When the receiver pushes the cornerback to about 25 or 30 yards, he breaks back upfield and slightly toward the sideline. Fred Biletnikoff has done this so expertly over the years that when the Denver Broncos drafted cornerback Louie Wright in the first round in 1975, the Denver papers wrote that he was chosen specifically to stop Biletnikoff. Wright did a decent job on Freddie's comebacks when we played them that first year, so we sent Fred inside on a post for a touchdown. The defense can attempt to take things away from you that way, but when they do, they're going to open themselves up for other things. On that play, as you see in diagram 28, the tight end runs straight up the middle of the field to keep the safeties from coming over to help out against our wide receivers on the sidelines. If the safety does, then the tight end should be open deep down the middle, but we'll get into that type of thing in the next couple of chapters.

Not only is the quarterback paid to throw the ball, he must spot these things in the defense and adjust to the different options he has at his command. He must make sure the receivers run their patterns so they are distributed evenly across the field. This spreads the defense out and you hit in between the areas where the defense has

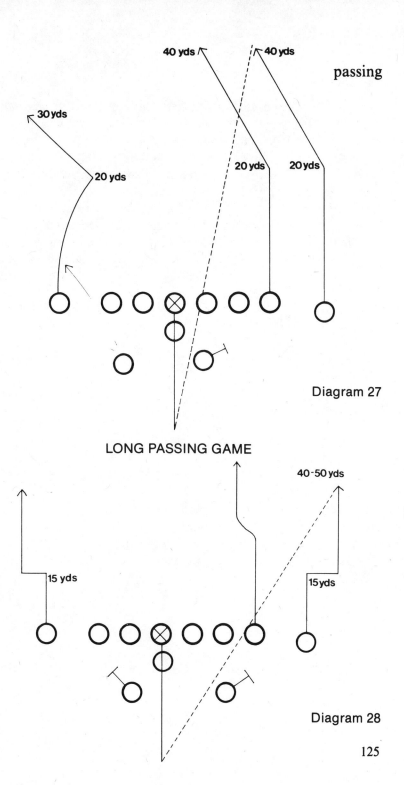

passing

40 yds
40 yds

30 yds

20 yds

20 yds
20 yds

Diagram 27

LONG PASSING GAME

40-50 yds

15 yds

15 yds

Diagram 28

125

its strengths. As pointed out earlier, you don't want more than one receiver in the same area because they will draw more defenders to that spot. The ideal situation is to get a receiver one-on-one with a defender. I believe that no one can cover any of our receivers consistently in man-to-man coverage. It's like in basketball when you clear a side for your hotshot shooter. If the other team is playing you man-for-man, you send all four players to one side and let Pete Maravich, Walt Frazier, or Rick Barry go one-on-one with the guy. We like to have Fred Biletnikoff or Cliff Branch going one-on-one with a defender. But not too many other teams will give us that type of coverage, going to zone defenses instead. But there are ways to break those, too, as we'll see next.

# chapter eight

DOUBLE-TEAM—Two blockers clear out one defender; or, two defenders cover one pass receiver.

FRONTS—Alignments used by the defensive line.

FUMBLE—The ball carrier is separated from the ball.

GAME PLAN—Predetermined blueprint a team takes into a game.

LINE OF SCRIMMAGE—Imaginary line running from sideline to sideline at position of ball on each play.

MISMATCH—A fast player being defended by someone slower, or a strong blocker on someone weaker.

PASSING LANES—Areas in a defense into which the quarterback tries to pass to his receivers.

PASS INTERCEPTION—A defensive player picks off a pass.

PENALTY—An assessment of yards against a team for an infraction of the rules.

ROTATION—The flow to one side or the other of a zone defense.

SEAMS—The open areas, or sweet spots, in a zone defense, which receivers and quarterbacks attempt to exploit.

SHORT YARDAGE—The offensive team has only a few yards to go for a first down or touchdown.

SLOT—The area between the outside wide receiver and the offensive line, where the other receiver lines up in "East" formation.

STRONG SIDE—The tight-end side of the offensive formation.

TENDENCY—Established pattern of what a team or an individual usually will do in a certain situation.

WEAK SIDE—The side of the formation opposite the tight end.

# attacking defenses

Pro football is definitely going through a defensive cycle. I don't know if it's exactly the same in high school and college ball, but I do know that a dominant defensive team can control a game all by itself at any level of the game. The defense is taking the play away from the offense. It's up to the offense to take it to the defense, go right at them, from the beginning. The offense must be on the attack, because it's tough to get things turned around once the defense establishes itself.

Look at the most recent powerhouses in college football—Oklahoma, USC, Alabama, Ohio State, Michigan, Notre Dame, and Nebraska. Sure, all of them possessed potent offenses, but they could play an awful lot of defense as well. It's even more evident when you look at the most recent pro champions. There's Pittsburgh, with its "Steel Curtain," which some people say is the best defensive team ever. Then Miami and the 53 Defense, Dallas and the Doomsday Defense, Baltimore's Deep Zone, the Kansas City team (which they say was picked out of a Sears and Roebuck catalog), and the legendary Green Bay Packers.

The only team I can remember winning the Super Bowl without a great defense was the New York Jets, but they played an excellent defensive game that day against the Baltimore Colts. Perhaps the defensive trend in pro football began in 1963 with the Chicago Bears. The Bears, also known as the "Monsters of the Midway," had a defensive reputation going back further than that, but that season they parlayed it into the NFL championship. Coach George Halas had a mediocre offense by NFL standards, but he had guys like Bill George, Doug Atkins, and Joe Fortunato on defense. They beat up quarterback Y.A. Tittle and the New York Giants in the Championship Game.

Pittsburgh linebacker Andy Russell says the guys on the Steelers' defense believe they can win any game, not just control it, all by themselves. They can; I've seen them do it. The first year the Steelers won the Super Bowl, they did it many times because their offense wasn't as consistent as it is now.

People say that the best athletes are being put on defense, but the good teams have great players on offense and defense. It's a matter of these outstanding players and what coaches are doing with them. I'm not putting down old quarterbacks who ran up great passing statistics 15 years ago and further back. Otto Graham, Norm Van Brocklin, Sammy Baugh, and all those guys were great passers, no question about it. But I would like to know I'm going to face all man-to-man coverage or just some basic zones every time I play. That's the way it was for a long time, even through the 1960s in the American Football League, which was strictly a passing league.

Things are much different now. It's more a game of cat-and-mouse. The quarterback is matching wits with the middle linebacker and the other team's coaches. Each team has coaches up in the press box observing the game and sending down plays and messages to the sideline by telephone. There's a lot of calculated guesswork. It all comes from studying films, making a game plan,

The coaches upstairs in the press box can see what the defense is doing better than anyone on the field, so when I come off the field after a series, I talk with them on the phones. They tell me what the defense is doing and we discuss how to attack.

131

reading defenses, and knowing a team's tendencies. It used to be a basic offense against a basic defense, and either they stopped you or they didn't. It has evolved into a science.

All plays are designed to work against basic defenses, such as the 4-3 used in pro football. But you're not always going to come up against basic defenses. When the defense switches to something else, the offense often must change with it. You can run the same play many times, but if the defense has overshifted its line to one side, all of your blocking combinations must change. Or, you may want to run back to the weaker side of the defense. Calling audibles is the quarterback's job, but everyone on the offense has a responsibility of reading the defense and suggesting alterations.

Every defense has some weaknesses, or at least places where the offense can attack and gain some ground. If a quarterback studies the opponent well before the game, or recalls what the defense did in a similar situation earlier in the game, he can often predict what alignment he will be facing and choose an appropriate play in the huddle. But so many times he'll come to the line of scrimmage and see something that indicates to him that the play he has called will not work. Or, he'll spot a weakness in the defense that he would like to exploit with another play. That's where the audible comes in. He must change plays.

I have to admit that I didn't get much into audibles until I came to the Raiders. Maybe 10 times in my career at Alabama did I change a play at the line of scrimmage. We could have done it any time we wanted, but I'm not a big believer in audibles. There is a large margin for error involved, because all 10 guys must pick up the change and make adjustments to their assignments in a split second. You're dealing with crowd noise and other problems, such as the distance between the quarterback and his wide receivers. I believe that the less you audibilize, the better off you are, but there definitely is a need for all teams to have such a system. There are times when you must have it. It can bail you out of trouble.

When the quarterback sees the defense ganged up in one area, he knows that there is a weakness somewhere else. If your offense is flexible enough to adjust, you're going to be in good shape. But the quarterback must also know in advance which plays will work well

The great Johnny Unitas of the Baltimore Colts (shown here in 1969) was one of the best at reading and attacking defenses throughout his career, but especially in a textbook drive to beat the New York Giants in overtime for the 1958 NFL Championship.

against a certain defense. This begins before a game when he studies a team's defensive tendencies and continues during the game itself when he notices a pattern in the defense or is told by a coach upstairs that the defense is using the same defense over and over in a certain situation. Then he'll be ready to attack it.

Say a team is giving you man-to-man coverage on first down and 10 every time. Earlier in the game you may have run against it, but when it came to passing situations, they switched to zone coverage, which is generally tougher to throw against. When you get the ball back the next time, you should pick your best pass against man-to-man coverage and probably go to your best receiver. Later, when the defense goes into its zone pass defense, you might surprise them by running into it. You must attempt to exploit the weaknesses of the defense rather than going into the teeth of it. We feel that no defense stops the Oakland Raiders. The only time we're stopped is when we do something to ourselves, such as a fumble, a pass interception, or a penalty. We believe that there are ways we can move the ball against any defense.

I never really sit down and play what they call paper games, diagraming certain plays against defenses, running against the weaknesses in them. But I do it in my head all the time. Now I don't want all you high school quarterbacks throwing away all your plays sheets and telling your coach that you've got it in your head. I've been doing this for 16 years, the last nine with the Raiders, so I know it pretty well. I'll do it a lot the last couple of nights before a game, just sitting there at home or in my hotel room going over things. I'll think, "It's second down and three, so they'll probably be in this defense, so if I want to pick up the first down I'll surprise them and throw." That's basically a good thing to do, but sometimes you might come up to the line of scrimmage and find they've lined up in something completely different from what you expected. They might have figured, "Oakland knows our tendency, so we'll switch on them."

I talk with George Blanda often about different situations and which plays work well. We'll be standing on the sidelines or in the locker room and one of us will say, "That's a good play, especially against this type of defense," or, "That play worked pretty well in

George Blanda was good at exploiting defenses in his years as a starting quarterback, and I've picked up a lot of things from him in discussions during both practice and games.

that situation during practice." This also helps, because if you talk about something and think about it, you remember it when the situation arises again. Many times I've seen something in a game, and thought, "We were just talking about that the other day." I'll call the play and most of the time it will go just the way it did in practice. That's where reading and attacking come in.

I know that many high school systems aren't sophisticated enough to change plays or even parts of plays in the middle of a game, but if you're going along and doing nothing, not gaining any yards, you have to do something different before it's too late. Give your game plan a chance, but when it becomes evident that it's not going to go, I believe it's the quarterback's duty to take the initiative to change things. Talk to your linemen to see if they can block their opponents in a different direction. Talk to your backs to see if they can make it to a different hole. Then go to the coach and explain to him what the others have said. In the last chapter I said a young quarterback shouldn't tell his coach, "I want to pass more," just because he's a good thrower and wants good stats. But when it comes to helping the team, if he has his own ideas, he should mention them. Communication is a big part of any team.

Many times, Fred Biletnikoff will come back to the huddle and tell me he can beat a guy a certain way, or tell me he's not going to run a pattern exactly the way he usually does because of the way the defender is playing him. Just because you don't have a play or a pass route in your offense doesn't mean you can't make it up right there on the field. I know that's been done before, and if it means the difference in a ball game, you do it. We haven't ever done that, because we have just about anything you can run in our offense. But before a game we practice the plays we think will work against the team we're playing that week. Many times, the big play will be one we didn't practice all week.

Reading defenses can be tricky because the teams try to disguise what they're doing, especially in secondary coverages. The way the defensive line positions itself at the start of a play is generally the way they'll play, though they do run different stunts with the ends looping and taking the middle rush and the tackles going outside occasionally. And they also jump around during the snap count.

136

Reading defenses once the play begins can be tricky because the other team will try to fool you before the play. The quarterback must study the defense on the move, while going back to pass, and understand the coverage before he throws the ball.

137

But the backfield is something else. They have so many different coverages they can run that it's easy to camouflage them. Some teams will line up differently every play, yet give you the same coverage three plays in a row. Another team might line up exactly the same and run different coverages every play. A team might line up in what appears to be a strong-side zone, and at the snap of the ball everyone runs in a different direction and it turns out to be a weak-side zone. These things make it tough on the quarterback and receivers because they must pick this up on the run, while the play is in motion. A quarterback might read zone on one side, but that doesn't mean he won't get man-to-man on the other side of the field. The quarterback can't keep his eyes on exactly where he wants to throw or the defenders will know. He has to read the coverage quickly, look away, and then come back there, hoping the defense is in the coverage he thought it was. If they aren't, he might throw the ball away intentionally, or eat it—take a loss—if he can't find another receiver or if the rush gets close.

I have read an article in which Joe Namath says that the reason defenses are controlling the game is that the 3-4 or "53" or "Orange" defense, with all its variations, allows the defense to clutter up the passing lanes downfield. I have to say that I agree with him. He says that if pro football wants to open up the game again, they should abolish these things, or at least limit the amount of substitution, so that a quarterback isn't looking at a different variation with different players out there on every play. Coach Madden calls this "situation substitution," and he's a great advocate of it.

In an "Orange" defense, as the Raiders call it, there are three defensive linemen instead of four, and a fourth linebacker replaces the other linemen. When all four backers drop off into the passing zones, that puts eight men back there to cover, at the most, five receivers. They can double-team your two best receivers and take their chances with the others. Teams also use a 3-3-5 against us, and others have even gone to six defensive backs. As I said earlier, we feel that Branch and Biletnikoff, plus our other receivers, can beat man-to-man coverage any time. They can also beat double coverage as well; they've done it before. But you can't make a living off that, throwing into coverages.

You can throw into coverage and get away with it sometimes, but here's what happens when you do it too often. A great linebacker like Lee Roy Jordan of Dallas will pick you off. You should attack the defense's weak spots most of the time.

There are times when we run right into the defense's strength because we feel we can just out-execute them. Throwing into double coverage is an example of that, and so is the way we run behind Gene Upshaw and Art Shell. People know our tendencies and are waiting for them, but can't always stop them. We just muscle them in short-yardage situations: Pete Banaszak, the best short-yardage

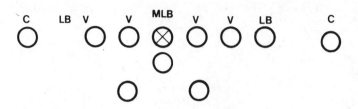

Diagram 29
Standard 4-3 defense

back I've ever seen, sticks his head in there for the first down or touchdown. You can do that against some teams, but not against all of them. The best thing to do is attack the weakest point of the defense.

We've diagramed some plays against defenses to show you how to find the weak areas. Since the defensive fronts and the secondary coverages have no connection, and a defensive team can run any front with any coverage, we will look at them separately. The first four diagrams (29-32) deal with fronts and how to attack them with the run; the last four (33-36) are pass defenses and how to dissect them.

Diagram 29 is the basic 4-3 defense, which is a very balanced defense. There are no particular weak spots as such, but any of your plays can work if you execute them properly. There are two linemen and a linebacker on each side of the line and the middle linebacker is exactly in the center. This defense brings the play down to our people against theirs.

An overshift strong, as shown in diagram 30, is simply a shift by the defense to the strong, or tight-end, side of the offensive formation. There is only one defensive lineman on the left side (of the offense), and the middle linebacker has moved one hole to that side. Their right defensive tackle now lines up on the center's nose, so that leaves only three defensive men on the left side, and two of them are linebackers. We're going to run a play that way, in which

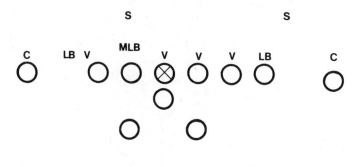

Diagram 30
Overshift strong

we have four offensive linemen, and we'll bring in a back for added blocking power to further make it a mismatch. The defense has overshifted this way because they believe we will run this way.

Just the opposite of the overshift strong is an undershift weak, as shown in diagram 31. The defense has shifted three linemen to the weak side, away from the tight end. If the tight end can take the linebacker inside, we run to the outside, and if he can take the backers outside, we go in against the defensive end and the middle linebacker. That's the weak spot in this defense.

The much-discussed 3-4 defense is shown in diagram 32. Some

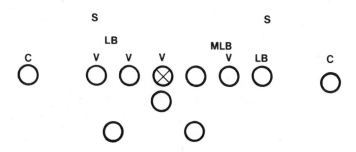

Diagram 31
Undershift weak

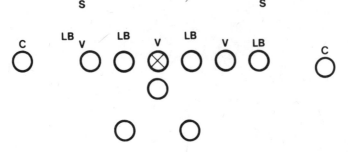

Diagram 32
3-4 defense

teams, such as Houston, New England, and Miami, have used this defense successfully against the run by blitzing at least one of the linebackers often. But in that case, it's not really a true 3-4. Many teams have gone to this because of injuries and others because their fourth linebacker is better than their fourth lineman. There are so many combinations that can be used in this defense that it sometimes becomes confusing. The teams listed above sometimes play the 3-4 most of the season, while others bring a linebacker off the bench. In our 4-3 defense in Oakland, we have defensive end Tony Cline, who can also play linebacker. This gives our defense an edge because we don't have to substitute to go from a standard 4-3 to the 3-4 with Cline standing up.

Though this defense is relatively new to the pros, it's just a variation of the old 5-2 Oklahoma defense that still is prevalent in college and high school football. The outside guys are just stand-up defensive ends with some pass responsibility. A lot of high school coaches use it because it's easier to find good linebackers than linemen. Cline and Ted Hendricks, our All-Pro linebacker, were the ends in this defense at the University of Miami in Florida during the 1960s. Monte Johnson, our middle linebacker, played that position at Nebraska. The weakness of this defense is the pass rush. We have five offensive linemen blocking against three defensive men. If a quarterback and receiver get enough time, they can beat any

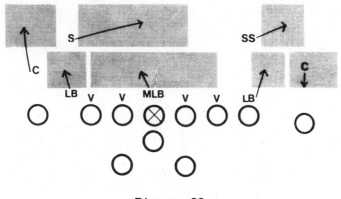

Diagram 33
Strong-side zone

defense. You can double-team two of the rushers. But if a team has three outstanding pass rushers, they can make this really work against the pass.

Moving on to pass defenses, we'll look at two zone coverages first. A zone is just a coverage in which each defender covers an area of the field rather than being assigned to follow one receiver everywhere he goes. Diagram 33 is a strong-side zone, with the defense rotating to the tight-end side. Their left cornerback rotates up, the strong safety rotates to the deep zone behind him, the weak safety takes the middle area, and the right cornerback covers the deep zone on his side. The linebackers then rotate to the opposite side of the backs. The weaknesses of the zone are that there are many gray, or open, areas. These are called "lanes," "seams," "slots," or "sweet spots," and you can see them in the diagram. You can play man-to-man a lot if you have great talent in the back-field, but if not, you can get away with the people you have back there by playing in zone. But great athletes can really make the zone work because they cut down these open areas. Instead of perhaps a 10-yard area, it becomes maybe seven.

In diagram 34, the defense is rotating to the weak side. It's exactly the same as the strong-side zone, only flopped to the other side of the field. The receivers try to get into the areas the defensive backs just vacated. For instance, when the strong safety rotates back deep,

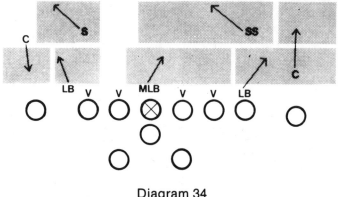

Diagram 34
Weak-side zone

the tight end or back may attempt to hook around the linebacker into the open area. This is again where our play fake comes in. If I fake a running play, the linebacker must respect it if we've been running well. That opens up the area between the linebackers and defensive backs even more.

Many people believe that you can't throw long against zone defenses, especially the kind of deep zones Don Shula used in Baltimore and took with him to Miami. I think you still can go long against the zone, but only on one side of the field, the opposite side

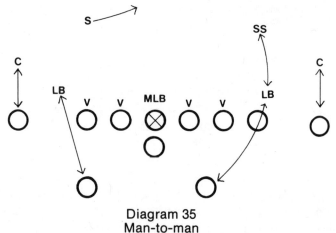

Diagram 35
Man-to-man

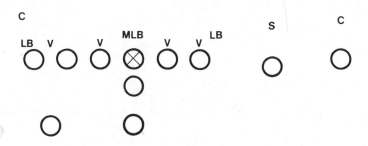

Diagram 36
East formation

of the rotation. But the zone is another reason passing games aren't what they were 20 years ago. People have taken to running the ball against zone defenses.

The Raiders believe that the zone can be thrown against, and we've done it consistently. One of the things we've done to eliminate some of these other coverages is to line up in what we call our "East" formation, as shown in diagram 36. We put both our wide receivers on the tight side of the field with Cliff Branch in the slot. Cliff gets double coverage, generally, from the safeties. They cover him inside-out. If he goes in, the inside safety takes him, and if he goes out the other safety takes him. What this does is leave Fred Biletnikoff, outside right, and tight end Bob Moore, lined up on the left, in man-to-man coverage. We also can run a back out against a linebacker down the left sidelines on the back side of our East, something that Clem Daniels did so well during his outstanding career in Oakland. There are only three or four coverages a defense can use when we line up in East. It's basically a passing formation, but we also have run to the tight-end side, away from our receivers, and gotten outside because the cornerback can't come up and give quick support against the run because he must respect the pass. He's alone on that side of the field. But whether we're running the ball or throwing it, when the Raiders are in East formation, we're attacking the defense. That's what an offense must do.

# chapter nine

ARTIFICIAL TURF—Synthetic grass surface used in many modern-day stadiums.

BROKEN PLAY—A play forced out of its normal pattern by the defense or an offensive mistake.

CHAINS—A 10-yard length of chain that designates the distance needed for a first down.

END ZONE—The 10-yard-deep area at each end of the field where points are scored.

FIELD GOAL—A three-point play accomplished by kicking the ball through the goal posts, above the crossbar.

FIELD POSITION—Spot of the ball on the field in relationship to the goal line.

GOAL LINE—The stripe at the beginning of the end zone, which if crossed by a player with the ball signifies a touchdown.

GOAL POSTS—The upright posts with a crossbar, in the back line of the end zone, through which field goals and extra points are kicked.

KICKOFF—A team puts the ball into play by kicking it to the other team from the 35-yard line (the 40 in high schools and colleges).

PUNT—One team kicks the ball to the other team on fourth down (occasionally third), when unable to gain a first down.

ROLL OUT—The quarterback drops to one side or the other rather than straight back on a passing play.

STICK—The pole at either end of the chain, one signifying the start of a sequence and the other the distance needed for a first down.

TOUCHDOWN—A player crosses the other team's goal in possession of the football.

TWO-MINUTE DRILL—A team runs plays without a huddle in the final minutes of a half.

# game strategy

Every time a team enters a game, it has a basic blueprint—called a "game plan"—prescribing how it would like the game to go from beginning to end. Unfortunately, things hardly ever go exactly the way you plan them. Football would be easy if they did, but maybe that's what makes the game what it is. There are too many things you can't control, or even know about, until you get into the game. You must get into the game first, see what situations arise, and then do what you must do.

There are so many variables that even though you begin a game following your game plan, problems arise that make you change different things even though you stick with the basic plan. Sometimes you must change even if you are ahead and controlling the game. There are such factors as: how the other team is playing you, the field conditions, the clock, your field position, and dozens of other little things.

You can begin preparing yourself for some of these things before the game. You should know your own stadium well, all the little peculiarities that go with it. You should know if the wind blows harder or differently in one area of the field, and if it's slippery in one spot and hard in another. The other team coming into your home park should be at a disadvantage, but you must know everything you can about your home field to take full advantage of that.

The Raiders have been accused of watering down the Oakland Coliseum turf several times, but that's a ridiculous accusation when we have a receiver like Cliff Branch. We don't want to slow him down; we want the field fast and dry. But the Coliseum is often wet, even when it doesn't rain, because it is below sea level and near the San Francisco Bay. I've been told that water seeps through from underneath.

When you travel to a different stadium to play, get to know what you can about the field if you practice there the day before the game or in pregame practice. Check for wet spots, especially along the sidelines and in the corners of the end zone. The direction of the wind is awfully important, too. The quarterback should make sure he can see the scoreboard from all areas of the field so that he can just glance at it during the game and instantly know the situation. I prefer digital clocks to hand clocks because the latter sometimes can be difficult to read. You can mistake 3:35 for 4:35 or 2:35. I've seen it happen before. You should also take note of which side of the field the chains are on. Make sure the field is marked properly, especially the end zones.

I've never been an emotional player because I believe the quarterback must keep his wits at all times, but even if you do play that way, you must stay aware of the situation at all times. If you need eight yards for a first down, on third down you must zero in on that stick whether you are the running back, the quarterback, or a lineman blocking for the guy who's trying to pick it up.

During the course of the game, you must do whatever is called for to win. Your team might throw 40 times or eight, but if you win the game it doesn't matter. The quarterback and coach must take into

When you need a first down, the player with the ball should zero in on the stick on the sidelines and concentrate on just getting that far before he thinks about breaking away. The same is true down near the goal line, only you go for the flag. Here I am just getting into the end zone in one of those Alabama-Tennessee classics.

Many people believe that you can't throw long against zone defenses, but we do it often with Cliff Branch, here scoring a touchdown. You can throw long against a zone only on one side of the field—the weak side, or the side away from the defense's rotation.

account how the other team's offense is doing against your defense to determine if you will have to play it wide open because more than 20 points will be needed to win, or to play a bit more conservatively if 14 or 17 might get the job done.

You must keep going back to a player who is having a good game against the defender he's facing. Cliff Branch beat Pittsburgh's Mel Blount for nine pass receptions and over 180 yards in the 1974 AFC

Cleveland's fine defensive tackle Jerry Sherk, a perennial Pro-Bowl player, seems to give us trouble every time we play the Browns. So we often handle him with two men, something we reserve for the very best players in the league.

Championship game. We kept going to him all day because we realized he was having that kind of game. In our overtime victory at Washington in 1975, Fred Biletnikoff turned cornerback Pat Fischer this way and that for nine catches and we just kept going back to him. It's like in basketball. If you're the Los Angeles Lakers, you have Kareem Abdul-Jabbar and you're going to go to him a lot in every game. But if you're the Golden State Warriors,

151

sometimes you go to Rick Barry, other times to Phil Smith, and on other nights to Jamaal Wilkes—whoever has the hot hand.

Field conditions have a great deal to do with how the game is played. Dick Romanski, our equipment manager with the Raiders, has several different kinds of shoes for us, depending on the condition of the playing field. Sometimes we change two or three times during a game if the conditions change. If it's a muddy day and the receivers can't run real good patterns the way they're called for, we'll alter them somewhat, or maybe throw more screen passes than normally. Games played in those situations tend to be low-scoring defensive struggles, so maybe you'll be more conservative, wait for the other team to make the first mistake, and take advantage of it. Or if you have a player who happens to excel on that type of field, you'll go to him, hoping he can break open the game. O. J. Simpson and Gale Sayers are players with reputations as "mudders," but they're great on any field.

If you normally play on a grass field and go to a stadium with artificial turf, it can change your game. Some players like it and some, or most, don't. But you still must play on it. It's like that in baseball, too. The pitchers hate AstroTurf because routine ground balls often roll through the infield for base hits. But hitters love it because of that and the high-choppers that also turn into hits. Infielders like it because the ball takes true bounces. In football, some receivers run good patterns on it and some don't. It makes some backs quicker than they are. Super-quick backs, such as Cleveland's Greg Pruitt and Terry Metcalf of St. Louis, can cause defensive players to have nightmares for days after a game on that stuff.

Wind conditions also are critical. If a quarter is coming to a close and you're in a field-goal situation, you might want to use a timeout to stop the clock so that you can kick a field goal with the wind. Or, you'll let the clock run out if the wind is blowing the other way. The same thing if you have a key third down coming up. Sometimes, you can't throw to one side of the field if the wind is blowing too hard. You must adjust your offensive plan. I've had interceptions attempting to throw into crosswinds, and against headwinds.

I've never played in New York's Shea Stadium because the Raiders haven't played there since I became a starter, but I know

Muddy conditions can change an entire game. Receivers must alter their pass routes if they can't run them properly and adjust to the conditions. Fred Biletnikoff, making a touchdown catch against Atlanta, is one of the best at this.

Extreme cold and snow also can change your strategy. You may not be able to grip the ball well enough to throw long passes, and your receivers may not be able to run certain patterns because of ice on the field. This happened to us in the 1975 Championship Game in Pittsburgh, when the icy conditions took away all of Cliff Branch's game.

from throwing in pregame warmups and just from watching the games that the wind there can be miserable. One end of the stadium is open and the wind comes swirling in there and seems to go every which way. Joe Namath knows the wind well there, but in some games, when it was really bad, he's just not thrown the ball much at all. That place has also been a real problem for field-goal kickers, but when Jim Turner was there, he had it down to a science. He just didn't seem to miss very often, even when the wind was at its worst. Candlestick Park in San Francisco is like that, too, but when John Brodie was playing there, he was the master of the wind.

Mile High Stadium in Denver is different from any other stadium we play in because of the high altitude. Turner is up there kicking for the Broncos now, and even though he may have lost something in his leg over the years, you never notice it in Denver. It may add a few years onto his career. You can really tell the difference with that rarefied air. But I like it. I can really cut the ball loose up there. I can't recall playing a bad game there. In the past three years, I've had eight touchdown passes in Denver. One went to Mike Siani for 80 yards and another to Cliff Branch for 60. In addition, there were several in the 20s and 30s, plus a 47-yarder to Branch that set up a touchdown and started a 35-point explosion in less than a quarter.

We've had good success with game plans in Oakland because we're a winning football team. I can't ever remember junking a game plan completely, but sometimes we've made big changes. We never go into a game figuring we're going to run a lot, but we've done that and won games. We never plan to throw a lot even though we're a passing team, but there have been games in which I've thrown 30 or more times—which I don't like to do—and we've won.

We played a game against Cincinnati in Oakland in 1974, in which Ken Anderson and I threw nearly 70 passes combined. I threw 42 of them myself because we were coming from behind the whole game and got into many passing situations. We won 30-27, so it was the right thing to do. But two years earlier, we played the Bengals in Cincinnati, the same two teams and two quarterbacks. We set several team rushing records and won 20-14. You use the things you're having success with and let the game situation dictate what you do. If I get in the huddle and my instinct tells me to call for a pass, I do. It's what I think the situation calls for.

We played a game in early 1975 against the Baltimore Colts, who had won two games the year before. No one realized at that time that the Colts would make the playoffs, so we were big favorites. We had to throw 34 passes to beat them 31-20, again because we fell behind early. We took them lightly. They played our run well and put on a fine pass rush, so it took a while before we took control. But we won the game, and that's how you judge things in football, not how you did it. I threw more passes than I wanted to or expected to, but they were enough.

Though I don't ever remember throwing out a whole game plan with Oakland, I can think of a few cases when we stuck completely with one for too long, perhaps because we've had so much success and are so confident. But if I had that 1974 playoff game with Pittsburgh to play over, I probably would throw 60 times. I threw nearly

155

30 times, but most of them were late in the game or on third down, obvious passing situations. We rushed for only 29 yards, and probably stuck with our rushing plan too long.

Injuries are another thing that can change a team's plans in midstream during a game. You may lose your star running back and have to change the plays you're running because his sub runs other plays better. Or you might have to go to a passing game. We got into a situation late in the 1975 season when all our wide receivers were injured and we ended up with tight ends Ted Kwalick and Warren Bankston playing out there while the others healed up for the playoffs. There are times when you have to play even though you're injured slightly. When my knees are hurting, trainer George Anderson just tapes me together and I go out there. I may try to get through a game without passing much, but when third and nine comes up, you have to pass.

You can prepare all you want for a specific game, but there are going to be times when you must go away from your preparation. That's where calling audibles comes in, something we have already discussed. This is something every player must be concerned with. When the quarterback comes to the line of scrimmage and either realizes that the play he called will not work or spots a weakness in the defense that makes another play pop into his mind, he must let everyone know he is changing the play. Sometimes he can also pretend he is audiblizing to make a certain defensive man move to another spot. Other times, usually in short-yardage situations, he may deliberately call a long count, hoping the defense gets overanxious and jumps offside. That's an easy way to pick up a first down.

The quarterback must make sure he is yelling his new play loudly enough for the rest of the offense, especially the wide receivers who are flanked out, to hear and understand. Sometimes your receivers may not even be able to hear your snap count and just move on the snap of the ball, so you must be sure they are tuned in for audibles. Broken plays can ruin an entire series.

In meetings and practices before a game, the quarterback goes over plays that should work against the upcoming opponent in all situations—short yardage, long yardage, first and 10, down near the

156

I've always called my own plays and that's the way I like it, even though plays are occasionally sent in from the bench. But even if the coaches are calling the play, the quarterback is in charge in the huddle and is the only player who should be talking.

goal line, deep in your own territory, whatever. When he gets into the game, he must select in just a split second the play he thinks best for the situation. At all levels of football, even in the pros, there are coaches who will call the plays for the quarterback, letting the players concentrate only on execution. Paul Brown did this for Otto Graham and Ken Anderson, two great quarterbacks. I've always called my own plays, and that's the way I like it, though Coach

157

Madden and the coaches up in the booth often will send in a play if they see something in the defense we can exploit. I have the option of using that play, or going with the one I have chosen, but generally I use their play because I respect their knowledge of the game.

You hear so much about being ready for a game, and certainly that's important. But once in a game you can't rely on that. If you can't adjust, all your preparation won't help you a bit. Much of this is dependent on your coaches. Our coaches are excellent at on-the-field control and this carries over to our players. It's perhaps more important to be a good coach on the field than it is to prepare your team to perfection. The Raiders are never in a situation we feel we cannot escape.

This is especially true in the final minutes of a close game. As I said earlier in the book, we have had great success driving down the field for game-winning scores with few if any timeouts left. Look at all the game-winning field goals George Blanda has kicked. Our coaches are very good in these situations, but sometimes you have to do it all by yourself if you have no timeouts left. We've done it under all kinds of different circumstances.

Three of those games stand out in my mind and in the minds of people who follow football. We won two of those games and lost one, but each time our offense went down the field against an excellent defensive team to score the go-ahead touchdown. The first one came in the 1972 playoffs in Pittsburgh. Daryle Lamonica was still our starter at quarterback, but we trailed 6-0 with around five minutes left in the game, and Coach Madden put me in. We had two chances. The first time, we didn't do anything and had to punt, but our defense got the ball back for us. Then we drove about 80 yards against that tough Pittsburgh defense, and I scored the touchdown on a 31-yard run when I was forced to roll out left on a passing play when linebacker Andy Russell blitzed. I kept on going right through the spot he vacated, 31 yards, to score. There was less than a minute remaining, but they pulled off Franco Harris's miracle to win. The Raiders believe to this day that Jack Tatum never touched that deflected pass.

In that game against Cincinnati in 1974 when I threw 42 passes and Ken Anderson nearly 30, we drove 60 yards in the final minute

Game preparation is a big thing in football, but sometimes it doesn't help you as much as being able to adapt during the game. Our coaches are great at this and at communicating with us. Here I'm in a sideline discussion with Coach John Madden.

When teams double up on wide receivers on the outside, that leaves the tight end with just linebacker coverage in the middle. When Cincinnati did this in the final minutes of our 1974 game to prevent us from getting out of bounds and stopping the clock, we went to Bob Moore in the middle for big gains in our winning TD drive.

without any timeouts remaining. They were jamming the outside against our receivers to prevent us from getting out of bounds to stop the clock, so I hit three big passes in the middle to tight end Bob Moore (now with Tampa Bay). Finally, I hit Mike Siani with about a 20-yard pass and he got out of bounds at the two with under 10 seconds remaining. Since we had connected with five straight passes moving down the field, we knew the Bengals would be all over our receivers with such little time left. So the bench sent in a running play and Charlie Smith scored with two seconds left. We won because we went against tendencies all the way down the field and used the clock well. If I had reached a point where I had to stop the clock, I would have thrown an incomplete pass intentionally. During that entire sequence (except for the final play, when we had time to huddle up), we went with what we call our "clutch" offense. This is our name for what is known throughout football as the "two-minute offense." All the plays are called at the line of scrimmage by the quarterback. It's tough to do because you can't be as flexible as you'd like with your offense and you must deal with crowd noise. Everyone must be able to hear the quarterback. I'll call out a play, such as "99, 2 swing," which is easy for everyone to understand. The 99 tells a certain receiver to run an *in,* while the other receivers have a complementary route to run in that situation. The 2 swing is a pattern the halfback runs, and the line knows to pass block because it's a drop-back pass. As soon as I call the play, I'll yell "Blue-go," to have the ball snapped. "Blue-go" is a phrase we use on the practice field at times instead of going through the full snap count. This is the only time it's used in game situations.

Clutch isn't the ideal thing to do, but it's necessary because you occasionally get into situations that aren't ideal. You need it because you just don't have time to go into the huddle to call a play. When I yell, "Clutch, clutch," everyone hurries back to the line of scrimmage and gets set to go. I believe that every team, even in high school, should have some way to do this.

The third game I'll always remember because of the way we won it was that 1974 playoff epic against Miami. The Dolphins had won two straight Super Bowls and had been there three straight years. It looked like they were headed there again when Benny Malone ran for a touchdown in the final minute. Again we used the middle of the field effectively and spent our timeouts wisely to move down the field. We came up with a third and three at the Miami 12 when I gave to Clarence Davis on a draw play. He ran five yards for a first down and we used our last timeout with just over 10 seconds remaining. On the next play, Davis made a spectacular catch in the end zone and we won. Vern Den Herder was pulling me down as I threw, and I didn't get as much on the ball as I would have liked. But I saw Clarence all the way and probably would throw it again if the same situation came up, even though many people said it was a lucky pass. Maybe it was, but very often you need luck.

People call these comeback victories miracles, but they aren't when you do these things over and over. The Raiders have a reputation for it, dating back into their AFL history. I could use 20 pages describing all the ones I remember. We know how to do it and we always think we can, even though we fail sometimes. We fell 15 yards short in the 1975 AFC Championship game in Pittsburgh, but we'll always feel that if we had had one more play we would have won. We had the play all picked out and I feel it would have been a touchdown. The thing that bothered me was that some writers and media people suggested that even though both teams played well, it would have been a shame for the Steelers to lose because they had been the better team for 59 minutes. They said it wouldn't have been fair for us to steal the game in the final one. All I have to say is, that's why they play the game for 60 minutes. Whatever you do to win, even in the final second, is fair. If you win because you built up an insurmountable lead early, or if you rally at the end, you deserve to win. In fact, it's tougher at the finish. But if you win, that's it. If you deserved to win, you would have won.

The quarterback's most important duty, other than calling the plays and running the offense, is to understand the workings of the clock and how to relate it to the game. In the early stages, there is no reason to rush or get excited if things aren't going well, even if you get behind, because there is so much time left. If you panic and begin to do things you normally wouldn't do, you can get yourself further behind and possibly out of the game before it's half over. As

162

With the Cincinnati defense set for another pass, we fooled them with this sweep for a touchdown by Charlie Smith and won the game with only a few seconds remaining. We did the unexpected on the entire drive and the Bengals couldn't stop us.

mentioned earlier, at the end of the first and third quarters, you might stop the clock or let it run, depending on whether you have the wind with you or will get it when the next quarter begins. When you get down toward the end of the half and are behind, it's impor-

163

tant to score if you get an opportunity because it can give your team the lift it needs at half-time. If you're going to receive the second-half kickoff, a score on each end of half-time can either put you back into a game or blow it open. If you have a lead coming down to the final minutes of the half, you might want to settle for a field goal rather than take a chance for the touchdown and possibly come up with nothing. Or, if you are in a perfect situation, you may go for the TD to take firm control of the game. Whatever is best at the time. If you are leading and have the ball deep in your own territory, you should control the ball, pick up a couple of first downs so the other team won't get another chance to score, and (if you get close enough to the goal) take one or two tries to score.

When the second half begins, it is important again not to get anxious, because there is still a lot of football left. But if you are behind, it can be important to score first. If you are ahead, you might play it a little close to the vest if you have the ball deep in your own territory, but you can't shut down your offense completely because sometimes it can be difficult to turn back on again if the game somehow gets close. Field position usually determines this. In the final minutes of the game, you must use your timeouts in spots where you would lose too many valuable seconds, especially if your team is spread out after a play and it would take a while to get into your clutch or two-minute offense. You should save your timeouts for these situations, use sideline passes if possible, throw an incomplete pass if no one is open, and know the players you can depend on in the clutch.

If you are trailing by more than a touchdown, you must score twice to win, but this isn't impossible. Dallas beat San Francisco that way in the 1972 playoffs on the day we lost to Franco Harris's miracle when Roger Staubach threw two touchdown passes in the final minutes because the Cowboys recovered an onside kick. If you need two scores, and get close once but come up to fourth down, you may want to kick a field goal to get within a touchdown and hope for another opportunity to score. These are situations that you don't face that often, but it's important to have ideas on what to do when they arise. If you are a quarterback, it would be beneficial to get together with your coach and the other quarterbacks on your team to discuss which tactics you want to use. On-field strategy is definitely one of the most important, yet overlooked, phases of football.

# chapter ten

It would be unreasonable to think that you could read this, or any other book about football, and then go outside and be able to apply all of the things you've read about right away. It takes a long time to grasp all of the things that go into successful offensive football, not to mention defense as well. But young players shouldn't worry about anything except going out and playing the game the best they can. The techniques and polish will come with time, as in anything else you stick with.

When you go through an organized program, the coaches will teach you the game slowly, in stages, so that you have a chance to absorb it over a period of time. Football is a game people play for fun, from the sandlots right through the pros. If you don't enjoy it, maybe you shouldn't be playing. I do it for a living, but I still enjoy

# summary

football as much as I ever did. I like going out to practice most of the time, even though the things you enjoy can get monotonous. When you can do something you enjoy, even if it's hard work, and do it well, that's what it's all about.

In addition to having fun, the main thing a youngster should be concerned with is learning and improving. When you are playing on a team, your coaches are there watching, and they can tell you what you need to work on to better yourself. Then, even in your spare time, away from the practice field, you can work on these things. Competition is a new experience when a player joins a team for the first time. He's going against other players his own age trying to be the best at a particular position so he can be a starter. This competition can be good for a boy's growth and development.

Losing teaches you that "winning is the only thing," as Vince Lombardi always said. This is our sideline after Franco Harris and Pittsburgh stole that 1972 playoff game from us.

168

I don't get very excited even when we win, but I get a great deal of satisfaction—something I feel inside. But you can always tell the look of a winner. Here I'm sitting on the bench after we have the game sewn up. Winning is something I'm used to because I've never played on a losing team.

Vince Lombardi said that "Winning isn't everything, it's the only thing." Football was his life, almost the only thing that mattered to him. I'm not exactly that way, but I pretty much agree with him there. I know people might argue this point with me, but I've never thought you get much out of losing. I've never enjoyed playing a good game and losing as much as just winning, whether I played well or not.

However, I don't believe that winning is essential at an early age. Kids from 6 to 10, maybe a little older depending on the individual, have enough pressures just growing up without having to handle the pressure of winning. They shouldn't have to worry, "What will the coach and everybody else say if we lose?" They should be having fun, not just in playing football, but in everything they're do-

169

ing. Too much pressure can force a youngster away from football. Kids should know the game pretty well before such pressures come along. They'll accept them by themselves.

As a person becomes older, the natural competitive urge comes out. It's greater in some than in others, and it comes out at different stages, depending on the individual. With maturity, a player wants to become better and realizes that winning is important. I recall that as I got older, I realized that recognition comes to those who win. People will tell you, "You're the best team," or, "You're the best back." The honors and laurels come to the winners. Not that you play just for them, but it's nice to receive recognition.

I guess one reason why football has always been such fun for me is that I've always been on a winning team. The worst seasons I've ever been through were the 8-4-2 years the Raiders had in 1970 and 1971. At Foley High and Alabama we were always 10-0 or 9-1, 8-2 at the worst. With Oakland, we're 12-2 or 11-3 in the regular season. I don't know what it's like to lose consistently, like five or six in a row. I've played on a team that lost three games in a row only once, in 1971, and although I was part of that team, I identify strongest only with the teams on which I was a starter. The first one was the 1973 team.

Sure, the Raiders always lose in the playoffs, usually in the AFC Championship game after we've won a first-round game, but that means we've gone 13-3 or so. That's awfully good and we're proud to get that far, but we strive to be the very best. We feel we are, even if we've never captured the Super Bowl. But what about the teams that go 2-12 or 4-10 and never make the playoffs? That's one way we deal with losing in the playoffs, but we still take it very hard. We know inside, however, that one of these days it will be different. The Raiders are going to win the Super Bowl.

Football is a team sport, and you win and lose together. But the quarterback is the focal point of the offense, and he usually gets the majority of the glory or the criticism, depending on whether his team wins or loses. I've always liked that type of pressure. It pushes a player to be a better performer. The quarterback calls the plays and is involved with the entire offense, and I consider that part of my job. If I had to play another position now, I think it would be a

170

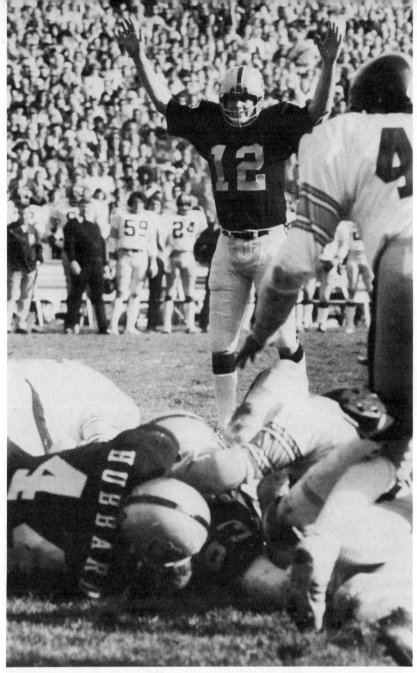

When the team does well, even if it's done with a running game, the quarterback gets a great share of the credit. He's the focal point of the offense. But he gets the lion's share of the criticism when things aren't going right, too. I like it that way. I'll take my chances.

little dull. Not that there isn't satisfaction that comes with being given an assignment and carrying it out. It's just that I've done this for so long.

The quarterback is responsible for the entire offense. He can discuss something with the left guard and the wide receiver on the right side. But you won't see those other two guys going over strategy together. I enjoy the responsibility, but how I do my job is related to the other 10 guys on the offense. I can't throw touchdown passes unless I get the protection and unless I have receivers who catch the ball. The offense is dependent on its 11 parts.

My feeling toward football hasn't really changed much since I was a teen-ager. It's always been a big part of my life. I couldn't have gone to college without it because my family couldn't afford it. I needed that scholarship. When I got into pro ball, I received an opportunity to make more money than most people in the United States, and to do it at a younger age. Without football, I don't know if I could have done that. And you can't beat doing something that you really like as a profession. It's certainly not like doing manual labor. What I have today, I owe to football. But on the other hand, football just gave me the opportunity. I had to take advantage of it. It's not the opportunity, it's what you make of it.

But even if I had never gone to college or played pro football, I wouldn't give up my high school football days for anything. I sit around and reminisce more about them than I do about what I've done in the pros and at Alabama. Especially when I get around the guys again, and I do often because I live there part of the year. There's a common bond of closeness I can't explain. I guess it's called camaraderie. To me, the high school days were the greatest, because there wasn't the pressure there is now. You could just play the game and have fun. I say that even though I enjoy playing in pressure games in the pros.

There is a spirit that surrounds football no matter what level you play on. In high school and college, it's more of a rah-rah thing. You have bonfires and rallies and you win for the red-and-white. We still have that in the pros, but it's inside. We handle it differently, but I feel the same about the Raiders as I did for the Foley Lions and the Alabama Crimson Tide.

I wouldn't trade my football days for anything in the world. I could have played in those early days when they worked five days a week and then went out and played with old leather helmets and no facemasks on Sunday. I think there are an awful lot of players who feel the same way. Football is a game of fun, but it's a game you must dedicate yourself to if you want to play it well. I hope you receive as much pure pleasure from it as I have.

# picture section:

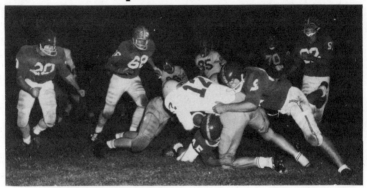

Stabler carrying the ball for the Foley High Lions.

With high school
coach Ivan Jones.

Though Stabler wasn't
a big passer at Ala-
bama, he still could zip
it out there with the
style that later would
make him one of pro
football's most accu-
rate and feared throw-
ers.

# the career of ken stabler

This scene tells the story of Stabler's last college game, a loss to Texas A&M in the Cotton Bowl, even though he ran for two touchdowns and completed 16 of 26 passes for 180 yards.

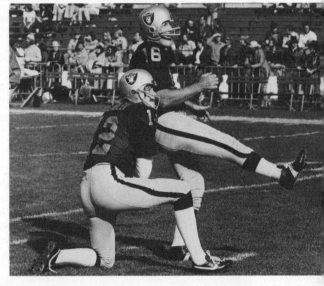

Holding for George Blanda's field goals and extra points has been a big part of Stabler's pro career, especially before he became the starting quarterback.

Stabler beats three Pittsburgh Steelers to the end zone for dramatic touchdown run in 1972 playoffs, only to be upstaged by Franco Harris moments later.

In his second game after taking over the Raider starting job for good in 1973, Stabler set what was then an NFL one-game accuracy mark with 25 of 29 completions against Baltimore, an 86.2 percentage. Included were 14 straight completions.

This is something that all Oakland fans and Stabler himself live with every day—the fear of another knee injury that would leave the Raider offense without its leader.

Kenny with wife Debbie during a public appearance.

Signing autographs, especially for youngsters, is part of a football player's job.

Stabler and co-author Tom LaMarre, on the job.

Ken Stabler was the most honored player in the National Football League in 1974. He won numerous Most Valuable Player, Player of the Year, and All-Pro awards. Here he receives the Newspaper Enterprises Association MVP award from West Coast Editor Murray Olderman.

# appendix 1

# ken stabler's winning record

## Foley High

| | | |
|---|---|---|
| 1961 | 10-0 | |
| 1962 | 10-0* | |
| 1963 | 9-1* | |

## Alabama

| | | |
|---|---|---|
| 1964 | Freshman team | |
| 1965 | 9-1-1 (including Orange Bowl win) | |
| 1966 | 11-0* (including Sugar Bowl win) | |
| 1967 | 8-2-1* (including Cotton Bowl loss) | |

## Oakland Raiders

| | | |
|---|---|---|
| 1968 | Injured, did not play | |
| 1969 | 12-1-1 (1-1 in playoffs) | |
| 1970 | 8-4-2 (1-1 in playoffs) | |
| 1971 | 8-4-2 | |
| 1972 | 10-3-1 (0-1 in playoffs) | |
| 1973 | 9-4-1** (1-1 in playoffs) | |
| 1974 | 12-2* (1-1 in playoffs) | |
| 1975 | 11-3* (1-1 in playoffs) | |

*Starter all season
**Starter last 11 games (9-2)

# appendix II
# stabler's college and pro statistics

## PASSING

| At Alabama | PA | PC | Pct. | Yds. | TD | Int. |
|---|---|---|---|---|---|---|
| 1965 | 11 | 3 | 27.3 | 26 | 0 | 0 |
| 1966 | 114 | 74 | 64.9 | 956 | 9 | 5 |
| Sugar Bowl | 17 | 12 | 70.6 | 218 | 1 | 0 |
| 1967 | 178 | 103 | 57.9 | 1214 | 9 | 13 |
| Cotton Bowl | 26 | 16 | 61.5 | 179 | 0 | 3 |
| **Career Totals** | **346** | **208** | **60.1** | **2593** | **19** | **21** |

## With Oakland

| | PA | PC | Pct. | Yds. | TD | Int. |
|---|---|---|---|---|---|---|
| 1969 | On taxi squad | | | | | |
| 1970 | 7 | 2 | 28.6 | 52 | 0 | 1 |
| 1971 | 48 | 24 | 50.0 | 268 | 1 | 4 |
| 1972 | 74 | 44 | 59.5 | 524 | 4 | 3 |
| Playoff | 12 | 6 | 50.0 | 57 | 0 | 0 |
| 1973 | 260 | 163 | 62.7 | 1997 | 14 | 10 |
| Playoff | 17 | 14 | 82.4 | 142 | 0 | 0 |
| AFC Championship | 23 | 15 | 65.2 | 129 | 1 | 1 |
| 1974 | 310 | 178 | 57.4 | 2469 | 26 | 12 |
| Playoff | 30 | 20 | 66.7 | 293 | 4 | 1 |
| AFC Championship | 36 | 19 | 52.8 | 271 | 1 | 3 |
| 1975 | 293 | 171 | 58.4 | 2296 | 16 | 24 |
| Playoff | 23 | 17 | 73.9 | 199 | 3 | 1 |
| AFC Championship | 42 | 18 | 42.9 | 246 | 1 | 2 |
| **Season totals** | **992** | **582** | **58.7** | **7606** | **61** | **54** |
| **Playoff totals** | **183** | **109** | **59.0** | **1337** | **10** | **8** |
| **Overall totals** | **1175** | **691** | **58.8** | **8943** | **71** | **62** |

# RUSHING

|  | No. | Yds. | Avg. | TD |
|---|---|---|---|---|

## At Alabama

|  | No. | Yds. | Avg. | TD |
|---|---|---|---|---|
| 1965 | 61 | 331 | .5.4 | 1 |
| 1966 | 93 | 435 | 4.7 | 3 |
| Sugar Bowl | 10 | 58 | 5.8 | 1 |
| 1967 | 111 | 364 | 3.3 | 5 |
| Cotton Bowl | 12 | 22 | 1.8 | 2 |
| **Career Totals** | **287** | **1210** | **4.2** | **12** |

## With Oakland

|  | No. | Yds. | Avg. | TD |
|---|---|---|---|---|
| 1969 | On taxi squad | | | |
| 1970 | 1 | -4 | -4.0 | 0 |
| 1971 | 4 | 29 | 7.3 | 2 |
| 1972 | 6 | 27 | 4.5 | 0 |
| Playoff | 1 | 30 | 30.0 | 1 |
| 1973 | 21 | 101 | 4.8 | 0 |
| Playoff | 0 | 0 | 0.0 | 0 |
| AFC Championship | 0 | 0 | 0.0 | 0 |
| 1974 | 12 | -2 | -1.6 | 1 |
| Playoff | 3 | 7 | 2.3 | 0 |
| AFC Championship | 1 | 0 | 0.0 | 0 |
| 1975 | 6 | 5 | -0.8 | 0 |
| Playoff | 2 | -4 | -2.0 | 0 |
| AFC Championship | 0 | 0 | 0.0 | 0 |
| **Season Totals** | **50** | **156** | **3.2** | **3** |

# index